Journeys of a Feeble Saint

Dr. Olen M.Evans and Debi Evans

authorHOUSE™

1663 LIBERTY DRIVE, SUITE 200
BLOOMINGTON, INDIANA 47403
(800) 839-8640
WWW.AUTHORHOUSE.COM

First published by AuthorHouse 10/11/05

ISBN: 1-4208-7536-1 (sc)

Library of Congress Control Number: 2005907174

Printed in the United States of America
Bloomington, Indiana

This book is printed on acid-free paper.

In memory of my parents

Miles Woodford Evans

1917 - 1966

Lola Belle (McCrory) Evans

1928 - 1966

Acknowledgments

All Scripture quotations are taken from the King James Version of the Bible unless otherwise indicated.

My most sincere thanks to my sister, Loretta Gallion, for typing the manuscript and offering valuable suggestions. Many thanks also to my wife for proofreading the manuscript, offering valuable suggestions, and co-authoring the book with me.

Special recognition is due the churches and pastors of Palestine Baptist Association for allowing me to experiment with preaching, learn to pastor and grow in the faith during the earliest years of my ministry.

Extra special thanks are due the Mt. Olive Baptist Church of West York, Illinois, where I was saved and baptized.

PREFACE

This is a book of journeys. It is not autobiographical. Many crucial events and circumstances of minor consequence carried me to the threshold of these major landmarks of my life. My encounter with God has not been as sporadic as these experiences may suggest. My fellowship with God is a lifestyle. It is not even daily. It is moment by moment. He is with me always. I daily read and study Scripture, pray, and commune with the Father. On special occasions, such as those in this book, I have received new direction and sudden periods of deeper growth.

By feeble I mean tottering and apt to fall at any moment. However I may be perceived by others, I have never felt I was particularly strong as a child of God. The writer of Hebrews spoke of "the sin that so easily besets us," (Hebrews 12:1). I think I have several such sins. I am feeble. I did not write this book to demonstrate my strength. It is dedicated "to him that is able to keep you from falling..." (Jude 24). He has consistently bolstered me--even forgiven me often--that

He may present me "faultless before the presence of his glory with exceeding joy," (Jude 24). I am often unsure of myself. I take life one step at a time. I do not know what tomorrow may bring. But "I know whom I have believed and am persuaded that He is able to keep that which I have committed to Him against that day," (II Timothy 1:12).

Above all, I am a saint. I know I am a child of God. "One thing have I desired of the Lord, that will I seek after; that I may dwell in the house of the Lord all the days of my life, to behold the beauty of the Lord, and to inquire in his temple," (Psalm 27:4). With all of my heart I give myself to God. That means tomorrow I will be more yielded than today. Tomorrow I will build on today's experience of walking with God. I will have better knowledge of how to please Him. Even my ability to try harder will be increased. Someday, by God's grace I will be as a bride adorned for her husband. Today, I am still getting ready for the marriage feast.

CONTENTS

Chapter One

Death

I woke up on the ground. I was barely twelve years old. Behind me was our overturned pickup truck. To my right lay my unconscious father emitting the worst groans I have ever heard. Several feet before me lay my silent mother whom I presumed to be dead. (She died only hours later.) To my left lay my lucid sister. Already on the scene were helpful people running to and fro. Before I heard the faint sound of approaching sirens, I had a brief conversation with my sister and then, against her insistence, I fell asleep.

Our family had attended my mother's family reunion that day. We were on the way home. It was Sunday evening, July 17, 1966. I realized as I awoke that we had been in a car/truck accident. The windshield of our truck had a large hole in the middle of it, through which my mother had been thrown, taking off the top of her head. I knew from my father's groanings that the accident was severe. As I awoke I attempted to stand up. A lady pushed me back down and assured me that everything would be all right. How far from the truth that was!

I turned to my sister and said, "We've been in a wreck. Why did this have to happen to us?" Without hesitation she replied (and I remember the words exactly), "Don't worry, Olen, we've got God on our side." My sister was solid in her relationship with God. She had been the leading factor in my being saved. She read her Bible daily. Even though I had been saved at the age of nine, I was not a godly youth. I had forsaken the Lord for my old habits shortly after my profession of faith. Consequently, I was not even sure I was saved. Doubt plagued me. My sister's word in that tragic moment pierced my soul. I was not sure that God was on my side. I knew He was on her side. Helpless, I laid back again to sleep a moment.

When I awoke next, I heard the faint sound of distant sirens. I knew the ambulance was coming for us. Soon they were loading us, my sister in the front seat, my father and I together in the back, my mother was taken in another ambulance. My father and I shared a room in the hospital emergency department. He repeatedly cried out for my mother. He bled to death shortly after arriving at the hospital. My sister had a slight concussion and a cut tendon on her foot. I was only slightly injured with minor cuts on my face and one on my back. A few stitches and I would be as good as new.

My soul was not so well off. I had been doubting my salvation. That was the most frightening and disturbing thing I have ever experienced. No one knew of my inner battles with God. But I had been spared from death when others around me had died.

My sister, three years older than I, was my stability. I had yet to learn that God was my rock and fortress, my refuge in the storm. But she served as God's witness to me. We had fought regularly as siblings at home but now it seemed we had nothing left worth fighting for and we have gotten along beautifully ever since. I admired her for her steadfastness although I laughed at her conversion. I secretly admired the fact that she read her Bible daily and was sincere as a Christian.

Death was not new to me. I had seen death in other automobile accidents. I was never sheltered from the reality of death. When I was eight my grandfather died. Because of old age and infirmity, my family had moved to the upstairs of my grandparents' house to help take care of them. My grandfather had become blind as well as feeble. One morning my mother awakened my sister and I to tell us Grandpa had died in his sleep. Two years later my grandmother died. She had suffered a long time with cancer and had been bedfast at home. I stood by her bedside and watched her last gasps for breath. Two years later I would watch my parents die.

By nature, I was not a rebellious child toward people, but I knew what it meant to be lost. I valued the honesty and integrity of my parents. Their values would ever become my own. My biggest problem was my mouth, I backtalked my mother, never my father. I had heard cursing all my life and I can remember cursing as long as I can remember talking. Alone in the yard one day, curse words fell naturally from my lips. I was less than five years old. I immediately felt guilty and I knew I should not say those words. I made a deliberate decision to continue saying them anyway.

One day I asked my mother what it meant to lie. She gave me the example that if I told her I went in the house and washed my hands when I had not really washed them, that would be a lie. I immediately went in the house, pretended to wash my hands and went back to tell my mother I had done so. As soon as I learned what lying was, I had to put it into practice. "When the commandment came, sin revived and I died" (Romans 7:9). From the earliest age, I proved myself a sinner. I was rebellious to God at heart.

I had a constant urge to exert energy. I possessed a great deal of pent up energy. I had drive, determination, and persistence to achieve. I could long endure adversity to get my desires accomplished. I could hold a grudge. I could out last my opponents in conflict. If I wanted revenge, I could bide my time until an opportunity arose to strike back. I could argue long after I knew I had been proved wrong. Energy ate at me like a frustration unless I had a project in which to pour myself. Later in life, I would become a workaholic and somewhat of a perfectionist.

My stubborn will would not be fully revealed until the Lord called on me to repent. As I grew to an older childhood, I felt the conviction of God's Sprit on my life. I was scared to death of Hell. I wished there was neither a Heaven or Hell. I hoped for annihilation at death. I knew I was going to Hell in my hopeless condition. I refused to share my fears with anyone. I prayed God would not take my life. I prayed that God would leave me alone for the moment but I feared He would never convict me again and I prayed for a later chance to be saved.

One evening when I was nine years old as we were going to bed, my sister told me that her friend's brother, who was in my Sunday School class, wanted to be saved. My sister suggested that I go forward with him the next Sunday morning. (In our churches an invitation is usually offered at the close of the sermon. Inquirers respond by going to the altar to be counseled by the pastor. We call it "going forward," "walking the aisle," "going to the front" and similar terms.) She thought it might be easier for him if I went forward with him and she encouraged me to be saved at the same time. She proceeded to ask me what I thought I needed to do to be saved. Before I could answer, she told me that if I thought it meant I had to believe that Jesus died on the cross for me, that was the right answer. I did not answer her. I never thought about the matter again until the next Sunday morning.

My friend and I were sitting next to each other in church, paying little attention to the message as usual. But when the invitation was offered I immediately began to think of what my sister had told me. I felt conviction but stood firm. My friend left his seat and walked to the preacher at the front. I felt momentary relief that I was no longer obligated to go forward for my friend's sake. Quickly the Spirit began to convict me. Again I stood firm. The next thing I knew I was moving toward the center aisle. I found myself moved there by God and

I was faced with a major decision. I could go forward and be saved or I could go out the back, pretending to go to the restroom. I made a conscious decision to go to the front. The preacher met me at the altar. I told him I had come forward to be saved. We knelt together at the front pew. He read some Scripture to me and asked me to pray for forgiveness of sins and ask Jesus to save me. I did. Suddenly a burden was lifted. I felt free. I felt a joyous sensation in my breast. My mother was there. She had followed me when I passed by her in the pew.

An instant change transformed my life. My sister noticed that my language improved. Unfortunately, I did nothing to nourish my faith and I soon fell back into my old habits. Doubts of my salvation plagued me. The fear of Hell tormented me once again. I was more miserable than ever. I was confused now. Before my profession, I at least knew where I stood. I wanted to tell my mother or the preacher about my doubts but I was ashamed. I kept the gnawing doubts to myself. It was an extremely lonely way to live.

That was my condition on that tragic Sunday afternoon. My sister had said, "We've got God on our side." My thought, yet unexpressed, was that I had no such assurance. I went through that awful experience wrestling with God instead of fleeing to Him for refuge and comfort. He comforted me anyway.

I never saw anyone mourn for the loss of my parents. I was not permitted to attend the funeral or funeral visitation. Even my grandmother made no mention to me of the accident. I dealt with the emotion totally alone. I determined to be strong.

I never wept at that time, except briefly when alone at night, for the loss of my parents. I suppose it was more from shock than anything. My pastor came to my new home and assured me that my parents were in Heaven. I accepted the inevitable. A few days later, I watched without emotion, as all our family's possessions were sold. I said a final goodbye to our pets and left behind the farm on which six generations of my family had lived and worked.

I made new friends in a new school and adjusted from country living to life in a small town. The adjustment was smooth. I never had nightmares. The transition was marked by the hand of God. I learned II Corinthians

1:3-5, "Blessed be God, even the Father of our Lord Jesus Christ, the Father of mercies, and the God of all comfort; Who comforteth us in all our tribulation, that we may be able to comfort them which are in any trouble, by the comfort wherewith we ourselves are comforted of God. For as the sufferings of Christ abound in us, so our consolation also aboundeth by Christ." As a pastor, I have comforted many bereaved and grief stricken people -- orphans and elderly, and every situation in between. I have learned that sometimes--usually--the best thing a friend can do in that situation is pay silent respect with his presence and say little or nothing at all to the grieving. Witty comments, catchy slogans and clichés are usually inappropriate. The doctrine of God's sovereign care is far more comforting than saying the loss was not God's will. It is comforting that a good God is in control. It is disquieting to think tragedy happens outside God's will and control. I had asked my sister, "why did this have to happen to us?" Her steadfastness, her resolute manner sunk deep in my soul and I have never questioned God since that day.

As far as orphans go, I was fortunate. I ended up in a Christian home. My sister and I were faced with a choice of where to live. We had several relatives that might have taken us but there were two serious offers from relatives. My sister had other options if we chose to be separated as some people advised. We finally decided to live with my mother's sister and her husband who was a deacon of their church. I had been accustomed to attending church, usually, just on Sunday mornings. Now we went three times a week. I was taught to tithe. Thankfully, I can say that I never had to learn to tithe. I was taught to tithe on my paper route income, later on the money I made from mowing yards and finally, when I turned 16, I tithed on the income of my first job. I have been a tither ever since and later I will show you how God has proved Himself faithful to pour out blessings.

Although I was in a good home, it would never be home. Although we were close relatives, I could never live to honor my aunt and uncle. My father, and I think my mother also, had been proud of me. I was the only heir to carry on the family name. A void was left that no substitute could ever fill. I lived to honor my parents. Everything was different. Lifestyle was different. Expectations were different. Approval and disapproval of activities was different. I never rebelled because I respected the home, but inside I never viewed the family as my family. That would be like forsaking my own parents. I never wanted to be like my aunt and uncle. I wanted to be like my own father and mother. While I am grateful for the home that was provided for me, I have never appreciated the sentiment that said my aunt and uncle raised me. I like to believe that my values and personality were instilled by my parents. I had parental guidance throughout my most formative years. It was their training I have always wanted to emulate.

I think my new family never understood me well either. I wanted to be part of a family, yet I was detached from the family. Whenever the family was introduced, I was introduced, not as family but as "staying" with them. I could never be fully received as much as I could not fully receive them.

My personality became suppressed, I tended to withdraw inside and became much more passive. Previously, I had been assertive in many situations. I willingly took second place to my cousin who was the same age as I was. It took years to regain my self-esteem.

There is a Father greater than all, and eventually I learned to appeal to Him for strength and refuge. "A father of the fatherless . . . is God in his holy habitation," (Psalm 68:5). Psalm 27:10 says, "When my father and my mother forsake me, then the Lord will take me up." How better to learn the Fatherhood of God than to have a wonderful earthly father who loved me and then a Heavenly Father who would bring me up in the nurture and admonition of the Lord. I would learn to call God my Father and I have never since been alone.

A feeble saint, yes indeed, but, "If we believe not, yet he abideth faithful" (II Timothy 2:13) and I was about to learn that lesson.

CHAPTER TWO

DOUBT

Doubt is the most terrifying experience I can imagine. When I was lost, I feared Hell, but at least I knew where I stood. With doubt, I not only feared Hell, I remained in a state of confusion. Doubt means that one is possessed of two minds. James 1:8 says, "A double minded man is unstable in all his ways." Doubt is complete uncertainty--constant wavering and indecisiveness. The lost man does not even consider his spiritual condition apart from the Holy Spirit's conviction. With doubt, I had enough knowledge of the truth to recognize the awfulness of separation from God.

My doubts started soon after my conversion. John said, "Hereby we do know that we know Him if we keep His commandments" (I John 2:3). I had made no effort to develop spiritually and had knowingly reverted to my natural state. Therefore, I had no assurance that I knew God. There was no incentive to confess my dilemma. Everyone at church thought I had been saved. I had been baptized and I was a member of the church. It was as easy to hide from reality as it was to fall back into complacency. I told no one of my problem. I assumed I was the only one who ever doubted. The Holy Spirit convicted me sorely. I wanted assurance but I did not know where or how to find it. Years passed. I became a teenager, lived in a new home, started a new school, and a new church. Still, my doubts haunted me. Invitation hymns were sung and I was miserable. I wanted to go forward in church but I stood firm against the desire. I spent sleepless nights wanting to talk to my pastor but I would not divulge my secret.

One Sunday afternoon, I remember it so well, I ordered a pizza before church with family members. I was extremely hungry but before the pizza arrived the

Holy Spirit began to convict me. I could not eat a bite. Every morning I awoke with a guilty conscience. It was not because I had done anything wrong the previous night. It was simply because my heart was not right before God.

I read Christian literature. I searched through Sunday School books. I read from a commentary, a Bible dictionary, and used a concordance my father had bought for my mother to help her prepare Sunday School lessons. I read from booklets given to me at church camp and Vacation Bible School

I read the Bible--the Roman Road and a marked testament of the Gospel of John. I used the concordance to look up verses on the word "saved." I read them all. To myself I said, "I have done that, I believe Jesus is Lord. I am sure He rose from the dead." Yet I did not know, if I died, whether I would go to Heaven or to Hell.

I have heard evangelists preach that if you have doubts, you are not saved. Some preachers go so far as to imply that, if they can make one doubt, they have done him the favor of exposing his lost condition. I believe a Christian should affirm faith wherever it is found. Some plant, some water but God gives the increase (I Corinthians 3:6). Jesus was gentle with weak faith. Isaiah 42:3 and Matthew 12:20 say, "A bruised reed shall he not break, and a smoking flax shall he not quench." To try to destroy feeble faith is spiritual disaster. To impugn the weakest faith is assault on the Spirit of Truth. I had doubts, yet had I not prayed to be saved? Certainly, I had a genuine desire to be saved--a desire as long as I did not have to expose my shame. I listened intently to sermons and Bible studies. Some people may have admired the apparent spiritual thirst of a young Christian, but mine was not spiritual development, it was a cry for help.

I later learned that doubt often implies a presence of salvation. The lost go through life oblivious to their condition. The believer earnestly desires more and more of God. Doubt does not necessarily indicate a lost condition because doubt is not the opposite of faith. The opposite of faith (belief) is unbelief. The doubter is not unbelieving but is uncertain. We are kept by the power of God through faith unto salvation (I Peter

1:5). We are saved by a simple act of faith. Our degree of faith waivers throughout life. Sometimes we are strong in our belief. Sometimes we question things we cannot explain (as John the Baptist did). When "we believe not, yet He abideth faithful" (II Timothy 2:13). Jesus prayed, "Keep through thine own name those whom thou hast given me," (John 17:11). He is able to keep what I have committed unto Him against that day. "He is able also to save them to the uttermost that come unto God by Him," (Hebrews 7:25). "Salvation is of the Lord," (Psalm 3:8, Jonah 2:9). "Nothing shall separate us from the love of God in Christ Jesus our Lord," (Romans 8:35). I am the Father's gift to Jesus and I belong to Jesus. "I have manifested thy name unto the men which thou gavest me out of the world: thine they were, and thou gavest them me; and they have kept thy word," (John 17:6). I am His--the sheep of His pasture (Psalm 100:3). I hear His voice and follow Him (John 10:4). I am held by the Father's omnipotent hand from which no man can pluck me (John 10:28-29). I am possessed by His Holy Spirit and that which was begun in the Spirit cannot be perfected by anything the flesh can do (Galatians 3:3). "He who hath begun a good work in me shall perform it to the day of Christ," (Philippians 1:6). Doubt does not make us lost. It simply means we have questions for which we need answers. As we mature in the faith, it is natural and healthy that we test our developing convictions.

I analyzed my salvation experience. I tried to remember the verses that the pastor read to me when I went forward at age nine. I tried to remember the prayer that I had prayed. I remembered the sensation of joy that was in my heart. Was that not evidence of salvation? I did not know for sure. I could not remember the verses the pastor read. I did not remember the prayer I had prayed. How could I be sure I was saved if I could not even recall my experience? I wished that the Heavens would open so that one could see God for a moment when he is saved. That would surely confirm salvation. I had yet to learn that we have a more sure word of prophecy than even the transfiguration of Jesus, Moses, and Elijah could bring. "If they hear not Moses and the prophets (Scripture), they will not believe though one rose from the dead," (Luke 16:31). Miracles that signify an experience do not require faith, but we are justified by faith (Romans 5:1).

Years passed. I was miserable. I was terrified. I would not get help. I stood firm against confessing my problem. One afternoon, alone in my room, studying verses of salvation, I exhausted myself. I fell on my bed and cried, "Lord, I have done all your Word says I have to do to be saved. If I go to Hell, that is the way it has to be. I cannot do anything else." Instantly I felt a peace and satisfaction. I had assurance of my faith. I knew Heaven was my home. I had trusted God to do what He said He would do and I thrust myself on Him. I learned that salvation is not based on remembering an experience. It is not based on what verses are read or even that any verses are read. It is not based on a prayer. It is not found in doing the right things. Salvation is based on Calvary. It is based on what Jesus did for me two thousand years ago; it is not based upon what I have done. By faith, I gave myself to God's hand. I relied on Him completely for my salvation.

Assurance of salvation grows within us as we live out our faith. I John 2:3 says, ". . . we know that we know him, if we keep his commandments." His transformation in us is indescribable evidence of the Holy Spirit who seals us with His image. And even "if our heart condemns us, God is greater than our heart, and knoweth all things," (I John 3:20).

After that, I found myself attracted to Christian friends. We went to church together and visited neighboring churches when they held special revival meetings. I developed an interest in prophecy. Of particular interest was the doctrine of the second coming of Jesus. I read books about it, talked about it, and hoped He would come in my lifetime.

I was driving home alone from a basketball game one night. I remember the spot exactly. The Lord spoke to me in an audible voice, rich and authoritative. I remember the words specifically. He said, "Do you believe Jesus is coming soon?" Before I could answer affirmatively, God said, "Well you better get to preaching it then." I knew I was alone in the car but I checked the back seat to be sure. I felt peace and joy in my innermost being.

That was not the first time I had thought about preaching. Secretly, I rather hoped He would call me to preach, but mostly because I wanted to tell people what I had to say about church, God, and religion. I would later learn to take my messages from God's Word and not force God's Word upon my feeble remarks. The call to preach brought with it a sense of awesome responsibility. My initial feeling of joy soon passed and I was left with a decision to make. I began my old habit of holding God at bay. I thought of how the acceptance of that call would affect my life.

I argued with God. I was only seventeen years old. If I accepted the call to preach, I would surely exhaust the Scripture before I grew old. Besides that, what would I say? I had only a few ideas put away in my mind. My friends--even family--would never understand my call. My life had not been consistent with a commitment like that. I would be the object of ridicule. I knew nothing about the ministry. I hated public speaking. I was not as intelligent as many people in the church. I offered all kinds of excuses, but God persisted. Once again, I felt the conviction of the Holy Spirit.

I was a senior in high school and at a time of my life when career decisions were being considered. I could not decide on a career. I attempted to join the military. I spoke with a recruiter and he took me to St. Louis, Missouri, for the physical. I was always slight of build but I failed to pass the physical because I was a few pounds underweight. I later learned that I had been measured several inches taller than I was and would have passed if the information had been recorded correctly. It was all of God. I was trying to defer my call for four years but God pursued me.

I took a job after high school in the town where I lived. It was a job I loved. I loved the people with whom I worked. I had a good future. God still pursued me. I loved my fellow employees but I was afraid they would make fun of me if I revealed any religious interest. They knew I went to church but that was all they knew of me spiritually. I felt they would not understand and I was afraid of any mockery that might come. I learned later my fears were unfounded.

God wanted me to accept his call and announce it publicly. After working only six months, I quit my job under the pretense of attending college. It was a move in the right direction, but I soon found a reason to fear the same mockery from friends at college that I had feared at my job. One Sunday morning, December 17, 1972, at church the invitation was offered. I was, as usual, convicted to go forward. The next moment I found myself being moved to the aisle. Once again, I was faced with the choice I had at my conversion. I could go out the back or I could go forward. I made a conscious decision to go forward. I immediately felt relief and peace.

Ironically, the ones I thought would make fun of me did not make fun of me. But the ones I thought would understand did not understand. As far as I was concerned, I was, from that moment a preacher. God called me. I had accepted. The matter was settled. The next Sunday I was invited to preach my first sermon. Opportunities arose quickly. I preached nearly every Sunday for the next two years while finishing my work at the local junior college.

I grew by leaps and bounds but all my doubts had not yet been settled. My salvation was somewhat confirmed by the fact that I had been called to preach. Would God call a lost person to preach? Surely not. There was, of course, the question of whether my call was genuine or if I was confused. But I was strongly impressed and convicted of the Lord's will for my life. The rapid growth helped me allay my doubts. I was not all I should be. I was a mix of Christianity and worldliness but I was trying hard and God continued to pursue me. A feeble saint was I, but I was soon to learn for all time that I was, indeed, a saint.

The next year, I transferred to a Christian college in Tennessee. I was away from home for the longest I had ever been at one time. I specifically went there to study for the ministry. God gave me a particular friend as a mentor, I needed him so desperately. He was slightly older than I was, had been a pastor, and was sincere in his desire to serve God and do right. I was particularly impressed with the limits to which he would go not to sin. His was no casual faith. Mine was more of a nod in God's direction, a nominal assent to a body of truth.

Above all, he wanted to be right with God. He knew more about the Bible when he came to college than I knew when I finished. We remain friends to this day although there is great distance between us. Everything I needed for spiritual growth was in place. I spent five wonderful years on that campus and graduated from the college and seminary.

In the Christian college, I learned that doubt was not unique to me. In a psychology of religion class, we spent some time analyzing Christian experience. As members of the class began to share their testimonies, I was astonished to learn that nearly every one had a similar experience with doubt. I have often preached on doubt, and when I do it rarely fails that a decision is made or someone comes to me confessing that they, too, had doubts or some similar experience. Satan wants the believer to doubt because it paralyzes his service. The truth sets us free.

Another problem with doubt involves a realistic understanding of what faith is. Faith is believing God. It is not a leap in the dark. I was in the dark until I experienced faith and now I walk in the light as He is in the light (I John 1:7). I have the light of life and His word is a lamp unto my feet, a light unto my path (Psalm 119:105). Faith is not walking in darkness. It is not accumulating all the available knowledge you can attain and then grasping for the uncertain and unprovable. Faith is based on the sure foundation of God's Word which is supported by many infallible proofs. It is obeying what you know is true. By faith Noah built an ark. He knew God's will and obeyed. So it goes with all the heroes of Hebrews chapter 11. They knew God's will and obeyed. Faith based upon knowledge produces obedience. And "faith without works is dead, being alone" (James 2:17).

To simplify matters, there are really only two things you can doubt. You doubt God or you doubt yourself. Either you doubt God--His ability to save or His willingness to save, or you doubt yourself-- your experience or your faith. Hardly anyone who is concerned about their soul doubts God Thank God, salvation is not based on your experience or your continuing faith. When we are faithless, He remains faithful (II Timothy 2:13). Salvation is based on Jesus' work on the cross.

One giant problem with doubt is that it excites the emotions. It is like riding in an airplane for the first time. You can know the safety record of air travel, the physics of a plane staying in the air, and the ability of the pilot but the tiniest element of uncertainty can produce fear. "Fear hath torment," (I John 4:18). "God has not given us the spirit of fear; but of power, and of love, and of a sound mind," (II Timothy 1:7). The emotional factor gets in the way of good judgment and the mind is rendered incapable of rational thought.

I would like to say my doubts were, at that time, settled once and for all, but not so. As I grew and matured in my intellect, I would again be faced with doubt. That seems to be a part of developing the mind of Christ. The issues are so important. We cannot help but grapple with other philosophies and ideologies. Believers are invited to try the spirits (I John 4:1), to prove God and thereby, to learn to trust Him only. I would wrestle with other doctrines in my youth. I would have to develop my own assurance for the faith I had been taught. I struggled with security of the believer, inspiration of Scripture and other major doctrines. The questions I had only served to strengthen my faith as "I gained a reason for the hope that was in me" (I Peter 3:15) and I found many infallible proofs to justify the orthodox position of the truth. As I grew, I learned to trust God more and more. For the questions that remain, I have learned to wait on the Lord. The secret things belong to Him, but I know I can trust Him even when I do not understand the details.

I cannot give satisfactory answers to the bereaved or the suffering for the deplorable conditions of this world, but I know God. I know He knows best. If He permits evil, it is so that He may bring a greater good from it. The evil Joseph suffered in being sold as a slave and imprisoned though innocent of a crime was overruled by God in that Joseph became the deliverer of his family in time of famine. His brothers meant it for evil but God meant it for good (Genesis 50:20). If, as Job, He never gives us a reason for our trials, I have learned that "They that wait upon the Lord shall renew their strength. They shall mount up with wings as eagles, they shall run and not be weary, they shall walk and not faint," (Isaiah 40:31). Surely, that is what God wants most. It is just that we wait. Waiting shows faith and waiting builds faith. "Wait, I say, upon the Lord," (Psalm 27:14). "Count it all joy when you fall into diverse temptations," (James 1:2).

Chapter Three

Division

In seminary, I learned all about God. In the pastorate, I would soon learn all about men. I had graduated. I felt ready to serve. I had never felt impressed to serve in a specific ministry. I never knew whether God would have me be an evangelist, a pastor, a missionary or would give me some other ministry. When I attended the first of the annual missionary conferences at school, I was afraid the Lord would call me to be a missionary. By the time I graduated, I rather hoped He would send me to a foreign field. That was apparently not God's will for my life. Doors began to open and I soon accepted the pastorate of a small church in the open country of a very rural community. I was a single pastor with very little experience and a whole lot of learning to do. I knew the Bible well enough to get by, but a class on personalities and characters of men had never been offered.

The church was small. My first Sunday everyone in the church was present. There were less than twenty in attendance. The vote to call me as pastor had been about seven for, none against. There had been no pastor there for four years. An interim had been serving. They paid me a full time wage. The church had been served by bi-vocational ministers up to that time.

I have always been enthralled by a challenge. All of the churches I have pastored have been on the verge of closing when I was called to the church. Each one had fewer than twenty people present on my first Sunday. The chairman of the deacons told me that he felt the church would close within ten years if something was not done quickly. I took that to mean I had free reign to serve. I was excited. I had all the time in the world and no responsibilities except the church.

I soon learned that not everyone was as excited about church growth as I was. I thought every member's goal was for their church to grow. I had strong evangelistic leanings. I visited and worked hard at visitation and study. The first year saw little growth but we did have a few baptisms. The second year was phenomenal. We saw attendance in the fifties. (That may not sound like much to you, but to reverse a trend of dying and then nearly triple our attendance was sheer success to me.) In the third year, the trouble came.

I always knew the chairman of the deacons was a descendant of Diotrephes (III John 9) but I did not know of what Diotrephes was capable. This man had a great deal of money and loved for others to know it. With his money he controlled church business decisions. He used it to bribe others so he could get his way. If he did not give his money, projects would not succeed. So others gave in to him. He intimidated people and made them afraid. He was proud, sat toward the front, looked down throughout the sermon, and when a crowd was present, he always made sure to get up, push out his chest and walk around. But he didn't have to get up. He is the only man I ever knew who could strut sitting down. We got along for the most part until the very end.

About six months before I resigned, he told some of his friends that it was time for me to go and that he would be asking me to leave. The friends told me of this. I told no one about his comment but I confronted him. He neither denied nor confirmed it. He was silent. I thought nothing more about it until he told some of our recent converts that we had all the people we wanted in church and we did not want any more. He told another soul winner that she was only bringing in the ones she wanted. He forbade me to use the church van to pick up people for church or for any other reason and that I was not to make any more visits for the church.

There were other factors involved that bothered me even more. A young couple in the church was getting divorced. I was accused of causing the separation. I was not guilty of that. However, I was guilty of being alone with the estranged wife and so rumors began. I was still single at the time. She and I had been good friends since high school. I had asked her to type information for an application for a Federal Communications Commission license to build a Christian radio station. She also typed my teaching outlines for church. The deacon took advantage of my indiscretion. Lies were told and scandal came. It is very hard to prove innocence in a matter like that.

I was embarrassed and hurt even though I am as vile as the accusation implies. William Cowper captured it well in the song <u>There is a Fountain</u>: "The dying thief rejoiced to see that fountain (of Christ's blood) in his day, and there may I <u>though</u> vile <u>as he</u>, wash all my sins away." It is rather peculiar that we, with the Scripture and hymns of faith, call ourselves vile, wretched, and worms, yet we get angry when personality flaws are exposed and we hasten to justify our character.

I went to the deacon's house one night to confront him because I had heard of a meeting held at his house. I had not been invited and had no knowledge of the meeting. The meeting was called to discuss my morality. He denied ever believing the rumors. Later, he confessed that he had used them to his advantage. I was angry the night I confronted him at his home. The confrontation was right. My motivation was wrong. I was more interested in how I appeared and what people thought about me than in how God appeared and what people thought about Him. In a quest to assert my righteousness, I had denigrated His glory. I learned that a pastor loses respect when he shows unbecoming anger. Ps. 37:8 (Holman Christian Standard Bible) says, "Refrain from anger and give up your rage, Do not be agitated -- it can only bring harm." I was a feeble saint on a journey learning to face problems.

I was secretly followed day and night in hopes that something I did could be used against me. I was harassed. Threats were made. The church's money was taken out of the bank and the church's account was closed. My salary could not be paid. Bills could not be paid.

Utilities at the church were ordered disconnected and the insurance was canceled. My opposers went around town asking that no one do business with us. I feared the phone calls, the comments, the threats. I am embarrassed to say I bought a gun. There were two people that, if they came to my house one more time,

I would threaten with it. A feeble saint was I. They never came.

I would not leave town because of the rumors but when I was told that no new members would be welcomed, I resigned. I had been ordained on the first Sunday of November and resigned on the last Sunday of November the same year. The other deacons individually sought me out later and apologized for their part in the conflict. They had been misled and misinformed by the chairman of the deacons. Two weeks before my resignation was final, the FCC granted me a construction permit to build the radio station I had been planning for four years.

I was not perfect in that situation, but as an older pastor said for my comfort, "You've gotta learn." After my resignation was effective, Diotrephes and his followers who left the church came back. That church remains small to this day. Most of those who attended when I was there are gone. None of our converts remain. They were not welcome. I have regretted the years I spent there, but not now. I made many friends with whom I still correspond. Everything was not bad. I did not get a degree there but I got an education.

During the recovery period of this conflict, I read John Owen's book, <u>Sin and Temptation</u>. I wept and prayed as I finished it and reflected on the shallowness of my life. The book spoke to me and convicted me of my sin. I had never considered the depth of the roots of sin in my life, the lightness with which I had regarded sin, the subtlety of the tempter, and the dire spiritual ramifications of it all. The lack of passion I had for righteousness was vividly revealed. I had truly been sincere in my desire to live for the Lord, but the content of faith can never be exhausted and God was moving me deeper into the knowledge of His grace.

A change came over me. The extent of the change would be revealed in time as application was worked out in experience. Sin, in all its forms, appeared most deplorable. I had to choose on which side I would stand. To be neutral was impossible. To go on following the easiest or most desirable path of the moment was not an option. The focus of my attention must be God.

I still falter, but at least I am conscious of my purpose. I hate sin not primarily because of what it does to me, but because of what it does to God. He is holy, tender, and sensitive to the slightest indignity. It cost God His only begotten Son to put away sin. How can I disregard such grace?

When I sin openly, I confess it publicly. When my sin is secret, I confess it privately to God. I have learned to confess sin the instant it occurs or as soon as God calls it to my attention. I do not wait for a particular prayer time or an exceptionally spiritual moment. I profit from unbroken fellowship with God as well as total freedom from guilt. The closer I get to God, the more spiritual I become, the more keenly aware I become of my personal sin. In addition, the more forgiveness I receive, the more deeply I love God (Luke 7:45-43). I have not attained any particularly high degree of holiness but "I press toward the mark of the prize of high calling of God in Christ Jesus," (Philippians 3:14). I desire with all my heart to be like Him and I shall be like Him when I shall see Him as He is (I John 3:2).

I learned to find comfort in the Scripture. I would capitalize on that lesson later in life (see chapter 5 on Devils). I read scholarly journals and biblical passages. It took a period of several months, or a few years, to regain enough confidence to pastor again. God did not leave me without a ministry. I would grow again as I learned to depend fully on Him. I had relied too heavily on the church and the people of the church. When they failed, my search for solid ground began. Learning to stand with God alone was the next lesson.

I did not come to that experience completely blinded. I had served as an interim pastor at a small church while preaching my way through junior college. A retired pastor was in the congregation. He had the sweetest wife, but he could be a cantankerous man. I think he was trying to help me, but he always met me at the door as people were leaving to tell me in no uncertain terms all that I had said and done wrong. It was loud, embarrassing and sometimes done in anger. I would go home feeling like a complete failure but by the next week I determined to do better and I went back to preach again. He was relentless. Every week was the same.

When I was pastoring my first church, he moved his membership to it and I was once more his pastor. I dreaded to see him join the church but he was different toward me. He was kind, helpful and I think he even liked me. I was never sure before then. When his wife died, before he came to my church, he asked me to assist with her funeral. He has since gone to be with the Lord. I will never forget those days of earning my place. He prepared me for confrontation. It had been hard to imagine much more difficult confrontation than those with which he was associated, but when I had to face confrontation of that deacon for his behavior, I needed the practice. Later, I would need it again as a manager of a business. Employee relations are not always easy.

I was never out of the ministry. Before my resignation took effect, I had my new goals set before me. The overwhelming majority of the church had supported me. They asked me to continue as their preacher. In fact, a regular business meeting was scheduled for the next Wednesday after my resignation was offered. A crowd was present. Members never before seen in church came to support me. The deacons were voted out of the church. I was formally asked to stay. The deacons immediately got up from their seats and walked out of the building, followed by their few supporters, mostly officers of the church. What hurt me most was the total disregard for my spiritual welfare on the part of those who told the rumor. They only wanted me out of their church. There was apparently no concern for me. It would take years to regain the security and confidence I had lost.

I was determined to face the rumor. I stayed in town and months later another church in the area called me as pastor. I had been recommended by a much older man who resigned for ill health. It was a bi-vocational church in which I could serve in conjunction with the radio ministry.

Seminary journals nurtured me back to spiritual health over the period of the next several months. It was hard to go to church, even to a different church. I could see personalities similar to the ones I had dealt with in my pastorate. I knew what those individuals would be like under pressure and I loathed them for what I believed they were capable of doing. That is when the Lord taught me that their sins and personalities were no more loathsome to God than my own. I was a feeble saint, but how else could I learn to organize people and help them function with one another? How else could I learn to control my eagerness and energy? Maturity is reached by learning patience through tribulation.

I have grown to love people again. My former love for them was shallow in comparison. I learned to love people while recognizing all their flaws. Now, I know better how to match personalities with tasks and other personalities. I know better how much to depend on others and what situations to avoid to prevent their failure. It took years to get to that point. My second pastorate was a chance to marry a bride and to resign in peace while being encouraged to stay. I love those people in that small church. The pastorate there was a short one. By God's design, I think it was for me more than for them.

Chapter Four

Dependence

I had only briefly visited large cities in my youth and that was on extremely rare occasions. My first year in the Christian college was my first experience of city living. Not only was the Christian campus atmosphere exciting, I discovered Christian radio stations in the city. There were three Christian radio stations on the air at that time. The concept was a relatively new one. Popular Christian music was just beginning to emerge.

My roommate, that first year, was a freshman broadcasting major. We tossed around the idea of starting our own station. I insisted that it be located in an area where there was no such station. I had some money as an inheritance from my parents. I thought it would be wonderful to introduce Christian radio back home. He would be the manager. I would be the owner. I guess we would live happily ever after in our dreams. The idea remained in the back of our minds throughout the remainder of my college experience and on into my seminary years on the same campus.

During my second year in seminary, and after considerable prayer, we began to pursue our dream more seriously. We knew nothing about the process of starting a radio station. We interviewed a few radio station managers and we sought advice from a corporation that assisted in start up procedures. According to the professionals, I had just enough money to start a station at that time. I understood that as a sign from the Lord to proceed with our plans.

We learned that the first step with the FCC would be rule making. That meant that a frequency had to be allocated to the city which we would serve. We had no city in mind. In those days, Christian radio did not exist in small towns, and success in them was thought impossible. Downstate Illinois, where I was from, is filled with only small towns. My only concerns were that we not be in competition with another Christian station, that we cover the area of my roots, and that we play mostly music. I, for one, listened to the radio primarily for the music and it seemed so many Christian stations broadcast one sermon after another all day long. Also, sound doctrine must be consistently broadcast at all times. We would broadcast only programs which were consistent with our own doctrinal statement. The station would itself be a ministry, not merely a vehicle for other broadcast ministries. I also wanted to broadcast without asking for money. Most of the stations I knew about asked for money much too often in my opinion. So we would be a commercial station and earn our finances by selling broadcast time to advertisers and programmers. I had strong views that the Gospel should always be given free of charge. All of our events, concerts, and content would always be without charge.

Furthering our progression of starting a radio station, we skipped a couple of days of school and drove about 400 miles away to search for an available city that would accommodate our dreams. We visited a few small towns in the broadcast vicinity and drove several miles in the area visiting various radio stations. We visited the largest city in our area first, but we found a Christian station already there. It was very poorly managed, worked with substandard equipment, and was extremely unprofessional on the air. Yet they had a Christian station and my first principle was violated.

We drove several miles to a town of about 12,500. It was in my home state of Illinois. We visited the only station in that town, which was a 50,000 watt country station. After being given a tour by the chief engineer and as we were leaving, we met a man at the door. He recognized us from college. He had recently graduated from the university we attended. Neither one of us had any idea who he was. When he introduced himself, he inquired as to our purpose for being in the area. He was the pastor of a local church there. We told him of our intentions and he said he had been praying for just such a Christian radio station and offered his assistance. We understood that as a sign from God to continue our pursuit. In time we would use him, though unsuccessfully, to locate a transmitter site. We were encouraged. After much prayer we decided to pursue that city as our city of license. Later, we discovered that the size of the town and the unusually progressive economy of the city made it an excellent choice for a new radio station. God knew best and directed us well in spite of our ignorance.

The next step was to find a specific location for the tower and transmitter. The FCC required an exact location for the transmitter site. The location had to be accurate to within just a few feet. We spoke with a real estate agent and checked out a few sites, but to no avail. One day, as we sat in the gymnasium of the college, a man came up to us. He was from that area and knew a pastor who had heard of our desires. He said his friend knew a man that had offered a piece of ground for our transmitter. We traveled back to Illinois to talk to him and he promised a tower site. We took him at his word and filed a rule making petition for that site on our FCC request. Over the four-year waiting period he gave up on us and donated the land (18 acres) to a church. We would eventually have to get permission from them before we could build our tower. (We were successful but that story will be covered in a moment.)

It took two years and considerable expense to file a petition with the FCC to allocate a frequency to that city. I prayed. I had determined to take things one step at a time, never completely sure if the idea was my dream or God's impression on me. The existing station in town contested our petition in various ways delaying the process. As doors opened, I would take a further step asking God to close doors if this was not His will. It was an exciting day when we received notice that a frequency had been made available in that city. By that time, I had graduated from seminary and was pastoring my first church in my home area.

The next step was to actually apply for the frequency. At that time, the application process was a lengthy one. It took several months to conduct and compile the required surveys and information. I spent several days and, in particular, I remember, one whole Christmas day working entirely on the project. Another two years would pass before a construction permit would be granted to us to build our radio station.

In the meantime, several changes occurred in the economy. We filed the first paperwork in May of 1978. By the time the application would be filed, inflation had ensued. My cash had less buying power and prices had soared. The amount that had at first been sufficient to complete the project was now only a paltry sum. I had no idea what to do. I just waited and left the finances in the hands of God just as I had left in His hands the granting of the FCC petition and application.

One evening the phone rang. The caller asked me if I would sell a particular piece of property I had inherited and if so, how much I would want for it. I quoted a price which I felt was completely unreasonable but without hesitation, he agreed to pay it. I now had just enough money to build the station. God had opened doors and answered prayer with matters beyond my control.

When the construction permit was granted, my former roommate moved from California to the city of our license. He had been working at a Christian radio station there since he had graduated. I had just enough money to buy excellent new equipment, but not enough to buy anything extra. We were happy with what we had and were ecstatic to sign on the air on October 4, 1982.

The station was operating but I was out of money. In fact, I had to take a modest loan to finish payment of some of the equipment. I also borrowed money from the bank to meet the first payroll expenses. That was the last time I ever had to borrow money. The first years were lean years. I had gone from possessing a large sum of money to having none at all. My income from the interest, which had been my livelihood while building the station, was gone. The station was not producing an income for me. In addition, someone had stolen my telephone credit card and charged $600.00 (a major sum when you have nothing). My gasoline credit card had been abused by a helper and I had over $1,000.00 to pay on it. I had no income and no food. God provided a job for me as a teacher at a local Christian school. They paid me the grand sum of $15 per day. That was next to nothing but it made ends meet if I was very, very careful. During the next year, I somehow managed to pay off my personal debts.

To ease the payroll, I let my secretary (now my wife) move into my house with her son so she would not have a rent payment. I spent nights sleeping on the floor at the radio station and often at a friend's house or my sister's house. It was not unusual that we had no food to eat and no money to buy any. We never discussed our poverty with anyone. God never failed. If we were without food, a friend would call at meal time and ask us to come to their house for supper. It happened over and over again. We never missed a meal.

At Christmas one year we had no money for gifts for my secretary's eight-year old son. It was the day before Christmas Eve when a check came for $80.00. We had a wonderful Christmas. That boy never realized how near he had come to a bleak Christmas. But then, "God is a very present help in time of need," (Hebrews 4:16). I did not have an extra fifty cents for a coke during that two years but looking back, I had everything I needed. I was a feeble saint but I learned to depend upon God for financial needs. I never stopped tithing on my $75.00 per week pay check.

I learned to depend on God for other things as well. Due to the financial hardship and several managerial blunders, my former roommate resigned his position, without notice, after only nine months. He liked to fantasize about the glory of media as though he was a celebrity. He told people he owned the station. I did not particularly object that people were confused about the ownership but when they offer business proposals it is important they speak to the correct person. He had convinced his wife they would be wealthy. Inflated ego is a common problem of many people in the media. He was no exception. Among other things, he had secretly singed a contract for $30,000 and I could not afford to pay it. Legally, I fought his authority to financially obligate the station and, after seven years of haggling, we settled for $4,800.00.

He gave me his notice of resignation on Friday and left me to work two twelve hour shifts on the air that weekend. A normal air shift is usually about four hours. It was grueling but, with the Lord's help and my soon to be wife's help, we made it. The fact of the matter was, that I was left alone to manage the station. I knew nothing of radio management. I had not even been in a radio station before we visited a few of them while desiring to start one ourselves. I was scared of the FCC rules and regulations. I knew only enough to know that a major mistake could cost me my license, and that would mean financial disaster. I read the entire section of 73H in the FCC Rules and Regulations until I understood completely the philosophy and requirements of the FCC. We were inspected at one point and passed with flying colors.

Another great problem existed with the church on whose property the transmitter was built. The church had voted to lease us a portion of their ground on which to build our tower. My manager and I met with the men of the church to determine terms for leasing a portion of the church's property. All went well and terms were settled. They would get a portion of broadcast time in exchange. However, my former roommate gave permission to the tower company to build the tower prior to the signing of the lease. We never could meet the pastor's requirements for us after that point. He and the church tried to control our staffing, our music, and virtually all that we did. I have never met a more unkind, unChristlike pastor. He threatened me. He screamed at me. He argued with me. I held firm to my convictions but he tried to intimidate me in every way. Moving the tower was hardly an option due to the large expense of the move and the lengthy procedure of getting FCC approval of a new site. We were constantly threatened with that proposal in spite of a formal letter of permission we had required from the church previously. We played a traditional, inspirational music format but the pastor and a few followers objected to fast songs, calling them rock music. We never played rock music, but some, especially Southern Gospel music was up tempo.

Our policy was to avoid controversial matters and to present solid truth. This pastor wanted to attack others of different persuasions. His spirit was divisive and offensive. The pastor threatened to tear down our tower. He even used his broadcast time to criticize the station. The program was immediately discontinued even though the broadcast time was an obligation of the lease. I offered to buy the tower and transmitter site. The pastor said they would never sell it to me. It was leverage to control our ministry. Twice I hired a lawyer to draw up a lease agreement according to the conditions upon which we had agreed. He refused to have his trustees sign it. He finally presented me with a lease, but the requirements were ridiculous and I refused to sign it.

When that pastor resigned, another came almost like him, but without as much credibility from his church. Tracts were even sent from some of that group explaining the plan of salvation because, as they said, my wife and I could not possibly be saved and play the music we were playing. They had all kinds of rules to follow in the church as well as in private homes. They were an extreme right wing sect, catering to the anti-social, anti-intellectual class of people. They got along with no one and criticized everyone.

The second pastor stayed only a short period of time before he split the church. During the absence of a pastor several years later, the church offered to sell me the four acres on which our tower and transmitter were located. What a welcome relief it was to own that property. The purchase was just in time for the impending sale of the station. A sale could have never been finalized under the original ownership conditions. God had allowed me a conflict that I might learn to allow Him to work in the hearts of my enemies. Isaiah said, "It was for my own welfare that I had such great bitterness, but your love has delivered me," (Isaiah 38:17 Holman Christian Standard Bible). "Blessed is the man that trusteth in the Lord, and whose hope the Lord is. For he shall be as a tree planted by the waters, and that spreadeth out her roots by the river, and shall not see when heat cometh, but her leaf shall be green; and shall not be careful in the year of drought, neither shall cease from yielding fruit," (Jeremiah 17:7-9).

I learned something else. I learned how to manage people as well as a business. The hardest thing I ever had to do was to dismiss a full-time employee. He had been with us since the beginning. He had a wife and three children. He was dependent upon the station for his livelihood, but he would not take instruction. I confronted him to no avail. Finally, I had to terminate him. He had been a friend, a confidant, and a good announcer until his ego soared out of control. I also learned to confront people sooner and to be quicker to share my desires, goals, and expectations for employees.

Perhaps the greatest thing I learned from radio was how to get along with business and professional people. Our finances depended upon it. I had been raised on a farm and then sheltered in a small town. I was intimidated by successful merchants, doctors, lawyers, and other professional people. Now, my livelihood depended on them. I soon learned they were very little different from me on the inside. The offer of Christ was needed by them as much as by me. I learned to be comfortable in their presence.

I also learned how to plan and execute successful promotion. Advertising is intended to build businesses. Special events we had conducted drew people by hundreds and even thousands. All this translated into promotion for church events and edifying the body of

Christ so that we could reach the unchurched and bless the current membership.

The radio station existed slightly more than eleven years. It only ended because of a devastating illness that precluded my ability to continue. I was now pastoring my third church. It was bi-vocational. I drove 25 miles one way to church for four years before moving to that town. Also during that time I began and completed my Doctor of Ministry degree. I was busy with a radio station to manage, a church to pastor, and a doctorate to complete. I ignored what I thought was only fatigue.

The Lord gave me some great Christian employees during those eleven years. They worked hard. I set the pace and worked as hard as anyone, and we were successful. My managerial skills were essentially nonexistent but I learned how to gather a staff around me and supervise people who knew more about their jobs than I did. I gathered many around me who were better at their jobs than I would ever be. Engineers knew technical work. Sales representatives could sell better than I could. Announcers were often far more skilled than I was. But they respected me for some reason and

I learned and benefited from them. Folks said we could never compete with the big secular station. Most people said a Christian station would not be able to survive in a small town. Others thought we would run out of songs and be playing the same thing repeatedly. Other stations tried to intimidate us and scare us. The eighty percent Roman Catholic town would not welcome an evangelical station readily.

It was not a lucrative business but I did not live for money. I only wanted enough money to continue the station and survive with my family. God gave us all we needed but we had to deepen our trust in Him experientially. God gave the money, the staff, the ability to manage the work, and the ability to work with people. I was a feeble saint, but God was able to keep us from falling (Jude 24).

Chapter Five

Devils

The fatigue I felt was getting more difficult to ignore. I often slept in my office for an hour or more during the afternoon. I got up at 4:00 a.m. to sign on the station so I just assumed that all of my activities had caught up with me. In the evening I liked to ride my bicycle with my daughter in a baby seat. If I particularly exerted myself, I would be ill until I took a nap, then all would be well.

A routine physical for an insurance policy indicated something else was wrong. I was directed to a nephrologist whose diagnosis was chronic renal failure. His words, "I can't give you any hope," were shocking.

I had been in perfect health. All of my grandparents had lived into old age. I never expected to be sick. The doctor suggested that a transplant would be necessary in about two years. Then he explained that, at that time, the life expectancy of the new kidney was an average of five years.

Cost of the anti-immune drugs was prohibitive, not to mention the cost of the surgery. I wondered if five years added to my life justified placing my family in financial disaster. My health insurance would not pay for experimental surgery but when they learned of my diagnosis, they placed a rider on my kidneys and refused to pay for anything kidney related. Since almost all of my problems could be kidney related, insurance paid for nothing. I considered the possibility of using the radio station as a vehicle to raise funds for the transplant. I waited. Circumstances improved when I qualified for Social Security Disability benefits and thus Medicare. The Psalmist said, "I've never seen the righteous forsaken or His seed seeking bread," (Psalm 37:25). I never had to ask for money. The sale of assets covered expenses during the two years of waiting that were required to qualify for the disability insurance.

Adjusting to a new lifestyle would be my next lesson from God. I knew I had to get more rest. During the next year I completed my Doctor of Ministry degree and thought it was about time, due to my illness, to find a replacement for my early morning radio shift.

The thought of dying was not new to me. For some reason, I always expected to die young. Illness had never entered my mind. Accepting this diagnosis was simply shocking, but I think I handled it fairly well. This would be a great lesson in accepting anything God threw my way. It led to the greatest joy I have ever known.

Fifteen years later, I still have not had a transplant, neither am I on dialysis. My kidney function continues to decrease, but at a very slow pace. I sold the radio station because of my inability to handle all of the stress. I was left with only a bi-vocational church. My family and I moved to an even smaller town--one of only 650 residents. We were determined to give our best to the church I pastored.

We had not lived in our new home very long when we began to have trouble with our telephone. Members of the church complained that they could not get through to us. The problems became so severe, so often, that we had to get a new number. Then, we found that our line was being cut on a regular basis. The incoming telephone wire ran down the side of our house from the telephone box and came inside through the basement wall. It was easy to splice the cuts but it was aggravating because it happened three or four times a week and continued for several weeks. We assumed it was pranks of neighborhood children. A friend of the church ran a new wire. He hid it and protected it so that it could not be cut. He left the old wire in place to serve as a dummy. Neither line was ever cut again.

During that time and after the new line was in place, we would find the phone module unplugged inside the house. There were times when the phone would be unplugged while I was resting in the next room. One day we got a phone call. My wife answered. The female voice on the other end asked, "Is this the Baptist preacher's house?" My wife answered in the affirmative. The caller went on, "Well, I hate Baptist preachers." She added, "You have a pretty little blond headed girl, don't you?" My wife asked her name, she responded, "I hope you know where she is all the time because I do." At that point the caller hung up. We took her words as a threat. Our daughter walked about three blocks to kindergarten and back every day. The high school was on the way, so her older brother would walk close enough to watch his little sister walk safely to school. We thought about driving her to school but we did not want to show any signs of being intimidated by the threat. We notified school personnel and the Sheriff's Department.

There would be another dozen calls or so over the next two years. The same female voice would say, "You know you're all going to die." Yes, we knew that, but we hoped it would not be as soon as the caller indicated. Our lives were threatened repeatedly. The Sheriff's Office authorized a phone tap which would be active for a month or so at a time. No calls came while the phone tap was in place, but they would start again as soon as it was discontinued. Everything we predicted came to pass. It was as though they heard every word that was spoken in the house. No calls came when I was at home but as soon as I would leave, another threatening call would be made. I suspected occult harassment but kept silent because I had no proof and did not wish to be classified as a religious nut.

I had some 500 mg antibiotic capsules that were left from a previous illness. One day I felt a bit of a cold settling on so I decided to take one of the pills to see if I could knock the cold. When I opened the bottle, I sensed a strong impression from God that I should not take the pills. I took one out to examine it and noticed that the letters and numbers on the pills did not line up on the ends of the capsules. I was not completely sure they were supposed to line up so I looked more closely and saw a faint substance like powder on the pill. I could tell they had been handled.

We took the pills to the pharmacy. They were opened and the pharmacist knew the contents was not an antibiotic. We took them to the Sheriff's office and he sent them on to the state crime lab. Soon the report was called back that the pills were filled with strychnine. Up until now we had dismissed the calls as idle threats.

The next two years were filled with harassment. Our dog's neck was completely sliced open from one side to the other. Two of our dogs were let out of the backyard and found dead on the highway. Perhaps this was coincidental rather than harassment, but the timing was suspicious. Within minutes after our leaving the house, the gate had been opened. We will always wonder if the dogs were killed before being placed on the highway because of the way they were found lying. They were found several blocks away just minutes after we left the yard.

One Wednesday night, our garage was set on fire. We discovered the fire quickly after it started and got it put out before any major damage was done. We had a bale of loose straw in the back of the garage for the dog house. It was burned. One rather tends to wonder, after that, if the house will be next.

One night we suspected that someone was in the back yard. It was very dark back there and easy to hide in the shadows. I went out, gun in hand. As I approached the fence, I heard someone scramble over it. I ran around the front of the house, not knowing which direction the intruder would run. As I got around to the other side of the fence he had scaled, I heard the door slam on the little rental house adjacent to our property.

We had been told that the man of that house had been bragging in a bar about harassing the preacher next door. We called the Sheriff at each new occurrence but there was no evidence pointing to anyone in particular. We only had our suspicions and we knew our neighbor had frequent bouts with the law. He also kept company with a woman in town that called herself a witch and dressed in only black clothing.

Another clue came when we found graffiti painted on our white house. Large black letters read, "Satan Lives" and in another place an upside down pentagon was spray painted in black. We examined the inside of the house and found occult logos and emblems placed on corners of pictures and plaques. They were barely visible but very real. Books on the occult disappeared from my personal library. A picture of Jesus in my study was turned upside down. Books were rearranged in my study. A long black hair was discovered on my pillow one night. My wife's hair is neither long nor black.

We lost track of the number of tires that were slashed on our cars. We found, on one occasion, a perfect circle of flower petals by the door outside. They had been taken from flowers on our kitchen table. Our cat had apparently been terrified. He would not even go into the bathroom where his litter box was. You could see fear in his eyes if he was forced toward the bathroom door.

My daughter was in kindergarten and first grade when all this happened. We sheltered her as much as possible, not speaking in her presence of our harassment. She told us one morning that during the night she had seen a man walking at the end of her bed and standing in her room. She tried to presume it was me but she knew it was not.

There was also a spiritual side of the harassment. Coinciding with this activity was a more spiritual battle for my wife and me. I faced temptations in ways I had never known before. Things that were completely out of character for me became enticing especially when I was out of town. For example, I was at a meeting somewhere and had a few minutes to spare. I went to a shopping mall. As I left a large department store, I passed a stack of catalogues on sale for $5.00 each. I have never stolen anything in my life, but the temptation to take one was overwhelming. It was as though I had to do it. I resisted with the brief opportunity I had to consider the decision and as Scripture says, "Resist the devil and he will flee from you," (James 4:7). The temptation was over as quickly as it had begun. I did not steal. I did not even pick up a catalogue.

I suppose I was tempted in every conceivable way. I came close to falling often, but a way of escape was always granted and the grace of God kept me from sin. I think I understand what it means to be tempted of the devil. Most of my temptations are from the flesh. This was an external impulse not the craving of the flesh. Sin was presented as the right thing to do. It was compulsive. I was a feeble saint.

I also felt periods of deep shadows come around me. Intense feelings of fear would descend. My wife and I both felt it. God said, "I have not given you the spirit of fear," (II Timothy 1:7). I had always interpreted the word "spirit" as an atmosphere of fear, but this fear had personality. Fear would come upon us suddenly and last sometimes for lengthy periods of time. A presence of evil could be felt around us and we often experienced it at the same time. It was a dense, forboding force of evil.

We heard sounds when no one was around. Doors would slam shut. Sounds of walking in other rooms were heard. Voices would be heard. My wife experienced a time of being held down in bed unable to move and a feeling of being strangled. She could not utter a word but would consciously call on Jesus and instantly be released. She was once pushed down by an extremely forceful hand. No one was around, but she fell hard enough to break her hand in several places. These were new experiences to us, but research on occult practices revealed them to be common occult occurrences.

We locked our doors when we left the house but we would find several items disturbed when we arrived back home. An affectionate picture of my daughter and myself disappeared from above the kitchen sink. We looked for it but could not find it until we went to bed. It was placed upstairs under my pillow. Numerous things were done to prove our house was penetrable any time. The intruders went everywhere in it. Various items would be hidden from us which were later found in the basement.

One day, we came home and found our family portrait with our faces all blacked out and a slash mark across my throat. When we were in revival at our church, a stuffed Easter bunny that belonged to my daughter disappeared. We later found it hung by the neck from the basement ceiling. There were countless miscellaneous signs of entry --never forced. Incidental items would be moved around. The chair in my study was often turned backward. Little, nonsensical, things all over the house were found. We never knew, when we came home, if the intruder was gone or was still in the house.

For a time, it was difficult to keep me in underwear. They would be taken from my drawer. Only personal items were ever stolen. I lost a necktie and our marriage license was taken.

I wrote a letter entitled "To my friends of the occult." I had it proofread for sweetness and sincerity by our evangelist. I assured the readers of my love for them and gave the plan of salvation. I taped it to the kitchen cabinet. The next morning a large kitchen knife was stabbed through the letter and stuck into the cabinet. It was not unusual to find things in the morning that were done while we slept upstairs at night.

One evening we came home from a high school basketball game to find all the burners of our gas range turned on but unlit. The house was filled with gas. Our son went in first and turned on the light. A spark would have ignited the whole house with a great explosion.

I suppose the most disturbing thing was the unlocking of our doors. We would come home at night, lock the doors and watch TV or read in the living room. When we got ready for bed we would check the doors again and find them unlocked. We never heard a thing.

We locked them again and the next morning they would be unlocked once more. This continued about five nights a week for two years. A friend of the church decided it was time for some new locks so he added dead bolts to all the doors. They were professional locks in addition to the others. He defied entry. Within the week, those locks, without even an outside key entry, were penetrated.

It bothered me that I could not keep out intruders who had threatened my family and specifically myself. No one ever saw anybody do these things. The neighbors watched. The Sheriff dedicated a week to watch at night from a hidden location. Nothing happened while someone watched. The state police and FBI came to interview us. I kept my gun handy for the first few months. I soon learned that spiritual warfare could not be fought with guns. I only wanted to protect my family. I was a feeble saint. I learned the hard way that it was God who protects us. We bought a well-bred Doberman to watch the house but he too was terrorized and fearful.

I sat up late, waiting in the dark for the avenger. Nothing happened while I watched. I became fatigued from sleepless nights and, when I did go to bed, I could not sleep well because of thinking and worrying about the threats. I feared mostly for my daughter. I even got to the point that I was so wired I could not sleep at all. Eventually, I had a complete nervous breakdown. I was hospitalized with anxiety. The doctor would not discharge me to go back home and insisted that I leave the area for a couple of weeks.

My wife called my college and seminary mentor. He and his wife agreed that I could stay with their family in North Carolina. The two-week stay was remarkably helpful but I felt I had forsaken my family, having left them alone in the house. The harassment stopped while I was gone. When I was able to come home again (six weeks later) the phone rang immediately. The familiar female voice simply said, "Tell him welcome home." The harassment began again.

I had tried to come home after only two weeks but on the way back, I woke up in our hotel room with an anxiety attack. It was severe. I had to return to a place where I felt safe. The two weeks became six weeks. My whole family moved down for the last three or four weeks. My friends were so comforting for me. Their church was very kind. They truly ministered to me. I was a feeble saint.

I did not tell anyone of the spiritual side of my warfare. I did keep the church abreast of the occurrences at my home. Some were scared. Some thought we were crazy. Some believed we only forgot to lock our doors at night--but twice a day for two years, under all this harassment? Some suggested we were being punished for some secret sin.

All kinds of advice was given. Many friends suggested we leave the house permanently. We would not give in to devils. I knew a lot of ministers from my service at the radio station. News traveled fast and people came from all over. Some wanted to cast spells and do incantations in the yard. I refused to allow them to do so because I knew God could take care of us without appealing to a Christianized form of sorcery. "The devil is as a roaring lion seeking whom he may devour," (I Peter 5:8). I did not think we could do better than simply trust God to deliver us. After all, that knife in the cabinet had completely missed my heart, which was the more desired target, and God had compelled me not to take those pills.

Through it all, I gained a new perspective on Scripture. While in North Carolina, I read First John so many times I virtually had it memorized. It meant so much and was such a comfort. I have never read the Bible the same way since.

It was also an opportunity to demonstrate the steadfastness of doctrine. I clung tightly to what I had believed and studied. I refused to give in to charismatic gifts which I felt were not appropriate. I lived what I believed Scripture taught and God did not fail. I never bound Satan, but God delivered my family.

Another lesson was the personal evaluation I did on myself daily. I searched my heart for any wicked way. I was driven to holiness. I surely did not want to be on the side of Satan. He scared me. I wanted to avoid sin and mediocrity. I also learned to recognize the tempter. I could see him now as the source of all doubts and evil. Truly he was an adversary. I learned absolute trust in God.

My neighbor was arrested and sent to jail on other charges. The harassment stopped immediately. The church had offered to buy the property on which he lived but it was not for sale. One day one of our trustees got a phone call. The owner passed away and his daughter said that if the church still wanted that property, she would give it to us. We wanted it. It did not take the men of the church long to tear down the house. Now that property is a part of my yard. God gave our enemies into their own snare. Just like God!

The harassment was ended but I still suffered from anxiety and my illness was also taking its toll. As a result of my nervous breakdown, I am left with a chemical imbalance in my brain that produces a serious depression. I am very much myself with medication, but on a psychological profile, I scored 37. Depression is diagnosed at 17. I had other lessons to learn. Disease would come to me. I cannot help but wonder if it was not an answer to an occult prayer to destroy me. It nearly did.

Chapter Six

Disease

The next two years brought out a boldness for holiness and witnessing. I left behind all fear and hesitancy when I spoke of Jesus. Talking of Him began to flow naturally from my lips. The subject does not have to be forced or rehearsed. I no longer worry about being too religious, but I do not believe I have become a religious nut. The saying goes, "One is so Heavenly minded, he is no earthly good." I would rather be Heavenly minded. I fear being so earthly minded I am no Heavenly good. I love God and I love the Bible. I am not the least bit ashamed of either and I am eager to discuss it. Conversation of Jesus just comes naturally because that is what I love. I speak often of both the Bible and the Savior to my wife and children as well as anyone else who will listen. Disease led me to this point.

I had anxiety problems stemming from my nervous breakdown. The inability to sleep, even with sleeping pills prescribed to me, nearly destroyed me. For some reason, I became unable to eat food. The starvation became so severe I could not tolerate the sight or smell of food. The thought of food nauseated me. My family ate their meals on the back porch to assist my repulsiveness to eating. I became malnourished. At first, I could eat only certain things, like Chinese food or seafood, but later I could eat nothing at all. My wife made me power shakes and soups but they did not sustain me. I reduced to 79 pounds, had no muscle mass, and had to be hospitalized on several occasions.

I also developed a bone marrow disease. I made no red blood cells. The cause of the disease was never determined. No diagnosis was ever made. I had every medical test and treatment imaginable. It could have been kidney related, autoimmunity, or something else. I had some of the best doctors in the state. I was prescribed extremely high doses of steroids to boost my immune system. They only deteriorated my hips and shoulder joints, and gave me osteoporosis. Those joints must all be replaced eventually. I ate well while on the steroids, but when I quit taking them, the starvation began again.

I survived on blood transfusions and, eventually, intravenous feeding. We spent thousands of dollars on treatment. I lost nearly all the cash I had from the sale of the radio station which occurred during and because of my illness. For the first time in my life I had to learn to be content while being abased.

The church gave me a leave of absence with pay for six months. They would have given whatever I requested. I passed out in the pulpit more than once but I kept preaching throughout the whole ordeal (except for the six months leave of absence). My doctor ordered me to end my career. I refused. God had called me to preach. I was a preacher. I could not quit preaching even if it meant the end of my life.

I began to develop adverse reactions to the blood transfusions. Doctors said they could do nothing else for me and that I would have about six months to live. That was eleven years ago. Prayer was offered literally around the world on my behalf. Today, I enjoy a healthy appetite, make red blood cells, and weigh over 200 pounds.

I was a feeble saint but I grew kinder in my illness and much more patient. I had to watch others handle my business affairs and take care of me hand and foot. I could not even get to the bathroom unassisted. I was completely dependent on my wife and God.

I learned to take whatever God laid on me and do it with joy. By nature, I was easily irritated and frustrated when disturbed, interrupted, or when my plans were changed. "The trying of your faith works patience," (James 1:3). "And not only so, but we glory in tribulations also: knowing that tribulation worketh patience; and patience, experience; and experience, hope: And hope maketh not ashamed; because the love of God is shed abroad in our hearts by the Holy Ghost, which is given unto us," (Romans 5:3-5). Waiting builds faith. I learned to be calm and allow God to work His perfect will in my life and circumstances. Once again, I refused certain practices of praying which I believed to be inappropriate. I did not accept an anointing with oil or laying on hands, except casually. I believed God was able to deliver me without ritual or aids to faith. I know what the Bible says about anointing with oil but I always understood that as a reference to medicinal treatment. The Good Samaritan poured oil on the wounds of the man on the Jericho road (Luke 10:34). "The laying on of the apostles' hands" (Acts 8:18 and 19:6), I believe, ended with the death of the apostles, just as did "the signs of the apostles" (II Corinthians 12:12), that validated the truth taught by them (Hebrews 2:3).

Trusting God for life itself has made me long for Heaven. In my illness, I eagerly anticipated being with God, my parents, and a host of converts and friends that preceded me in death. I was a little disappointed when I got better. My first thought was that I would have to go through all this illness again some day. My joy never left me. I am "ready to go, ready to stay, ready to do thy will" as the song says. Whatever befalls me, I am ready to bear with the grace of God as my sufficiency. Trying times are still not easy times but I have "joy unspeakable and full of glory." I am not sure yet what all "full of glory" means, but I have a good start on "joy unspeakable." How I love life, but I love God more.

I went into surgery completely relaxed for three hip surgeries, including my first hip replacement. When I awakened after my hip replacement surgery, people were all around me. Someone was bagging me. I had gone into respiratory arrest. I knew things were not going well but I had complete peace, trusting God for whatever happened. I fell back asleep. The next time I awakened I had been intubated. My hands were strapped to the rails of the bed. With all the medical tests I have had, nothing has been more uncomfortable. I writhed in the bed. I could not be sedated because I had been too heavily sedated already. The surgeon told me later that the recovery was a miracle. He and many others had prayed and he volunteered that it was God to be thanked.

I was completely uncomfortable. I knew things were not well but I had complete confidence in God. I was on the ventilator for sixteen hours and spent three days in the intensive care unit, but I recovered fully. I had already sufficiently dealt with the death issue. Jesus said, "If a man keep my saying, he shall never see death" (John 8:51). Death to self, with which I had grappled in my illness focuses one's affection on things above where "our life is hid with Christ in God," (Colossians 3:1-3).

Jesus prayed that we would have "His joy" (John 17:13). It is a Heavenly joy not based on parties and celebrations. It is a joy Jesus called "fulfilled" in us. It is not natural. Jesus is the object of that joy and He is its subject. It is a joy not based on life's experiences. God alone is that joy. It came to me as I despaired of life. I could not be full of myself and be full of His joy. When I denied myself a love for this temporal life, He produced the fruit of the Spirit which is love, joy, peace, longsuffering, gentleness, goodness, faith, meekness and temperance (Galatians 5:22).

Jesus found joy in God. So shall we. I learned to rejoice always.

The disciples were poor, weak, and helpless. They were needy. Sin had marred them and sorrow dimmed their vision. Jesus prayed for their joy. All but one died a martyr's death. Theirs was pure joy. That is worth clinging to which holds contempt for death.

That joy is a joy that delivers a witness. It exudes confidence and boldness.

About three months after I was given six months to live, I woke up one morning feeling well. I knew I was better. I began to eat. Food tasted good. It did not make me sick. I had started, without drugs, making red blood cells again. Doctors were amazed. They confessed it was a miracle. I still need a kidney transplant and only one hip has been replaced, but I am active again and fully enjoying life. Whatever time the Lord gives me on earth is pure grace.

In my weakest days, when I could not get out of bed, I would lie alone and pray. I wept often thinking about the heart break it would be to my young family to see me go. That is why I sold the radio station. It had been my dream and my wife did not enjoy the work as much as I did. I knew it would be hard for her to sell what had been my dream after I died.

I wept for my daughter. I did not want her to be fatherless as I had been. I prayed that God would not take me until she was on her own, at least out of school. (She graduated high school in the spring of 2004 and I preached her baccalaureate service.)

I wept for my wife. How hard it would be to lose a husband only in his early forties.

I never wept for myself. I did not feel robbed of life. I was not angry. I accepted the disease as of the Lord. How the community and church were amazed when I recovered! They knew--even lost people admitted--that God was at work in their midst. It was evident that "Truly our fellowship is with the Father and with His Son, Jesus Christ," (I John 1:3). The cure was as mysterious and unanticipated as the illness itself. Following two years of suffering, I woke up one morning, felt better, and started eating normally. The central line and tubes through which I had been fed and treated were removed. I gained weight from that day and I made a complete recovery from the bone marrow disease and eating disorder. Doctors were amazed. They pronounced the recovery a miracle. They had sent me home to die. God had other plans.

Those days of communing with God and getting answers to prayer are priceless. "When I am weak, then am I strong," Paul said (II Corinthians 12:10.). The church grew during that time. Evidently God increased it at that time to prove it was He and not me who builds the church. We have grown steadily since. The 17 we had our first Sunday together has grown to over 100. Admittedly, we are not a big church. We are in a small town, but we are not barely hanging on. We have a great spirit and a great God. The church is all I care about. Personal business decisions are over. Financial stress is passed. I live in a small rural community and spend my hours studying God's Word. My life is so very rich!

Like Mary, I sit at the feet of Jesus hearing His Word. I believe that is the one needful thing (Luke 10:42). Some people have asked if I can remember all I study. I confess that I cannot. I reply with an illustration I heard years ago about a woman trying to carry water in a wicker basket. By the time she reached her destination, the water had all seeped through the cracks. Someone chided her for her wearisome toil. She responded, "Yes, but look how clean my basket is." God's truth may be poorly held in this vessel of clay, but the one who studies will be "clean through the word" (John 15:3).

My next experience would involve the sorting out of life's opportunities, developing a philosophy of life's ministry, and following through on decisions.

Chapter Seven

Decisions

I thought I would have to find a more lucrative pastorate when I recovered from my illness. I could not support my family on my current salary. The income from the radio station was gone. The property I inherited had been sold and used for medical expenses -- and taxes. I supposed the Lord was preparing me for a move to a new location. It has been my policy to let the Lord place me where He wants me to serve. I have never sent out resumes unless requested to do so, but I felt particularly favorable about one specific church. I had a resume sent to them. They called me for discussion but nothing further materialized. I came to realize God wanted me to serve where I was. I love it here. I love the people and, so far, they seem to love me.

Friends question my decision to serve in such a small place. One of my professors heard me preach and commented, "I hope the Lord puts you in a place where he can use you." I believe the Lord has and can use me here. Evangelists that come to our town nearly always try to find a bigger church for me to pastor. If I served in a remote village in Africa, they would commend me for my dedication. To serve in a small community in America seems to send the message that you are not really very capable after all.

Small churches have always encouraged me. The church in which I was saved never ran more than 30-35 in attendance Sunday morning. The church where I went between my first and second pastorates only ran about 100. I have always felt a need to give something back to small churches and, so far, this is where God has used me.

Some people say I should be in a place where I am busier exercising my gifts and have more responsibility.

I am flattered that anyone believes I am suited for a greater challenge and larger congregation. Alfred Edersheim was criticized for serving a congregation beneath his capability. However, the quiet repose enabled him to produce four great volumes, including his monumental classic, <u>The Life and Times of Jesus the Messiah</u>. I am not an Alfred Edersheim, but I serve a people just as important to God as any other congregation. I know nothing in Scripture that commends or congratulates a church for its size.

Pastoring a small church may seem like easy street to some folks. Make a few visits and you have covered your bases for the week. Prepare a couple of sermonettes and wait for another Sunday to roll around. Let me correct your view. First of all, it takes as much preparation to preach to five as it does for fifty, five hundred, or five thousand. The same intensity is built into every preacher who genuinely wishes to do his best in the pulpit.

Furthermore, it is harder to grow a church of twenty than it is to grow a much larger congregation. There are fewer workers. The workers you do have do all the work, not just a single ministry or two. There are no programs in place to attract prospects. Visitors who come are not impressed. There is little or nothing for youth--a key ingredient to attracting families. There is virtually no music program and anyone who is willing to sing is welcomed to do so regardless of the quality of his voice or style of music. Sometimes it is even a treat just to have a pianist. The Sunday School has a wide age span in the children's classes and usually not more than one or two adult classes. Teachers are not plentiful and often not qualified.

Money is a constant issue. The few good givers you have are tapped out if you offer any mission projects at all. The building may not be in good repair or modern, or if it is that is where all the money goes. The pastor's salary is glaringly the largest budget item and still he must sustain himself with another income.

The same people hold the same office forever simply because there is no one else to do the work. They often become bored and exhausted because the work does not grow or has declined. Workers often sense no drive to work harder because what they are already doing is good enough "for just us."

Spiritually, converts are few and rewards are sparse.

Of course, there are positive points. It takes fewer members to make a convert and churches in rural areas reach a larger percentage of their community than city churches.

The pastor, regardless of his giftedness, is seldom sought by his denomination, praised for his efforts, or considered for outside engagements. Many small churches have had so many pastors come and go that they have granted the leadership power to a dominant figure in the church. Every decision must be pleasing to him before the pastor can move the congregation forward. Even so, power struggles often lead to forced termination. When the church wants a preacher rather than a pastor, sustained growth seldom happens. If the pastor is to lead his congregation, that congregation must untangle the leadership knot and give the power to the pastor.

The pastor of a small church handles all the weddings, funerals, and hospital visits. He makes all the calls and does all the counseling. He has no assistants on whom he depends. There is no margin for error. To lose a family is devastating. It requires a special person to serve an extremely small congregation, just as it takes a special person to handle an extremely large congregation. The call of God on both their lives is just as certain and compelling.

I do not believe it is easy to pastor a congregation of any size, but I do want to dispel any theory that suggests the small church is a small responsibility. Most of the small church pastors I know do all the work of a pastor of a larger church while holding down a full time job. Then they are scolded by others with the idea that if a church is not growing something is wrong with its leadership. Maybe, as with rural churches, the community is declining and the members have moved elsewhere. Isaiah was told to preach "Until the cities be wasted without inhabitant, and the houses without man, and the land be utterly desolate, and the Lord have removed men far away, and there be a great forsaking in the midst of the land," (6:11-12). Often, a bigger church with more to offer is so attractive that the area's prospects are attending it. I am not making excuses for lack of growth or letting dead churches off the hook, but I would like to insist that a lack of growth is not necessarily anyone's fault. Some churches are doing all the right things and yet just do not grow. The fault is not their own. God gives the increase. Theoretically, it is impossible for every church to get bigger forever. We are fishers of men. We cast the net. The choices for the catch are up to God. If we prepare ourselves well and serve God faithfully with a pure heart, that is about all we can ask.

I live in Brownstown because this is where God has placed me. I do not believe advanced education or skill in Scripture or leadership automatically entitles one to a more influential, prestigious, or lucrative position. I did not move to Brownstown because it was a charming little community with which I was favorably impressed. My first impression of the village was not good. The community was not attractive. There were several vacant, deteriorated, and even abandoned buildings on the main route into town. A number of homes near mine were in disrepair and occupied by immoral people. I moved my family to Brownstown because there were Christian people who desperately wanted a leader who was called of God. I rejoice that God gave me a place to serve Him. That gives me great joy. There are also a lot of good people in our congregation. God has blessed our service here. That is all that matters.

I had a conscious decision to make in my ministry. The fatigue I experienced precluded a full day's strenuous activity. My service would have to be limited. I spent a majority of my time visiting prospects in my first pastorate. I believed that was the fastest way to reach people and draw them to the church. I was no longer able to study adequately and visit extensively. I had to choose between proper study habits and visitation. I opted on study, believing that to nourish and feed the church and its guests was a priority. After all, God had called me to preach and those who come to church truly need to hear a word from God. The apostles had said that they should devote themselves "continually to prayer and to the ministry of the word," (Acts 6:4).

Paul told Timothy that those who labor in word and doctrine are "worthy of double honor, " (I Timothy 5:17). The decision paid great dividends. Our church never fails to receive guests on Sunday morning and we continue to baptize converts consistently.

Worldly men have asked why God puts all these challenges on one man. They believe I have done nothing to deserve the trials. That thought is the essence of the first temptation of Jesus in the wilderness. Satan said, "If you are God's son, command that these stones be made bread," (Matthew 4:3). In other words, God's Son does not deserve such harsh treatment. Even Christians have asked, "How much is one person supposed to take?" Some of our brothers preach a prosperity Gospel that teaches that a child of God should be free from suffering. It is when you break the alabaster box that a sweet fragrance fills the room. Crush the tiny atom and a great bomb explodes. Crush the child of God and the sweet character of Christ can be seen. "I reckon that the sufferings of this present time are not worthy to be compared with the glory which shall be revealed in us," (Romans 8:18). "Many are the afflictions of the righteous, but the Lord delivereth him out of them all," (Psalm 34:19). Let us "follow in His steps," (I Peter 2:21). The blood of the martyrs is the seed of the church.

To suffer as a Christian is the highest honor. It shows the world we have something better, something real inside. "Count it all joy when you fall into diverse temptations," (James 1:3) It is a delight to "partake in the fellowship of His suffering," Paul said (Philippians 3:10). That does not mean we delight to suffer. Suffering is truly agonizing. It is not fun. But to be made conformable to Jesus is sheer ecstasy.

Tribulation is how God makes us able to serve others. II Corinthians 1:3-4 says, "Blessed be the God and Father of our Lord Jesus Christ, the Father of mercies and God of all comfort who comforts us in all our tribulation, that we may be able to comfort those who are in any trouble, with the comfort with which we ourselves are comforted by God." We best comfort the bereaved if we have grieved, the sick if we have been ill, the helpless if we have been helped. What we have received from God we freely give to others. So we, as Paul, "endure all things for the elect's sake," (II Timothy 2:10). For the world's sake, Paul said, "I think that God hath set forth us the apostles last, as it were appointed to death: for we are made a spectacle unto the world, and to angels, and to men. We are fools for Christ's sake, but ye are wise in Christ; we are weak, but ye are strong; ye are honourable, but we are despised. Even unto this present hour we both hunger, and thirst, and are naked, and are buffeted, and have no certain dwellingplace; and labour, working with our own hands: being reviled, we bless; being persecuted, we suffer it: Being defamed, we intreat: we are made as the filth of the world, and are the offscouring of all things unto this day," (I Corinthians 4:9-13).

We are in the world to learn what sin really is so that we may truly praise His absolute holiness. Because of the knowledge of sin, we learn what self is really made of. The character of God may be justly appreciated. God's loving, tender, forgiving and keeping nature may be rightly enjoyed. We learn the long-suffering and goodness of God through the knowledge of sin. Sin may come to us as well as its consequences but this greater good of knowing God is ours. Nothing is really evil if it cannot separate us from the love of God. All else "works together for good to those who love God, to those who are the called according to His purpose," (Romans 8:28).

"Who shall separate us from the love of Christ? Shall tribulation, or distress, or persecution, or famine, or nakedness, or peril, or sword? ... Nay, in all these things we are more than conquerors through him that loved us. ... Neither height, nor depth, nor any other creature, shall be able to separate us from the love of God, which is in Christ Jesus our Lord," (Romans 8:35, 37, 39).

Temptation reveals ourselves. Failure empties us of ourselves. Difficulties humble us. Disappointments separate us from a love of the world. Pain chastises us.

Trials let me see myself. I can better understand that my motives--even the best laid ones--are not what my deceitful heart has led me to believe they are. Most every action--noble as it might be--has somewhat of a selfish motivation attached. I find that I seek my own good before I think of God's honor. I am a feeble saint indeed, but the weak things of the world confound the things which are mighty," (I Corinthians 1:27). God's strength is made perfect in weakness, (II Corinthians 12:9). "It is good for me to be afflicted so that I could learn your statutes," (Psalm 119:71 HCSB). In the third verse of <u>Amazing Grace</u>, John Newton summarized it well: "Thro' many dangers, toils, and snares, I have already come. 'Tis grace hath bro't me safe thus far, and grace will lead me home."

I am not writing this book to glorify myself for enduring hardships, tribulation, or sufferings. If the grace of God had not sustained me, I would not have endured. I am not wanting anyone to feel sorry for me. I have not suffered nearly as much as some people. "You caused me to experience many troubles and misfortunes, but you will receive me again, even from the depths of the earth. You will increase my honor and comfort me once again," (Psalm 71:20-21 HCSB).

I have never suffered directly for Jesus. I have never really been persecuted by men. Having read <u>Foxe's Book of Martyrs</u>, I realize I have done nothing at all. I am not saying that I am an example to anyone. Some believers claim they get victory over certain sins as though they have risen above temptation. "Let him that thinketh he stand take heed lest he fall," (I Corinthians 10:12). I am not wishing for pity, or applause, or amazement at my endurance. But look how God has transformed me, increased my joy, and developed a Christian character which manifests the fruit of the Spirit.

Conclusion

I love God! These words may seem a bit obvious from a minister who has served since 1972 and has been a Christian since 1963. But hear me out. It is a new concept for me. Oh, I suppose to some degree I always loved God. I was taught in Sunday School that I should love God, but in light of my new found love, I feel the old love was quite inadequate and very selfish. I loved the God of nature for the beauty of life. When I accepted God's call to preach, I loved the church. When I graduated from seminary, I loved the Bible. I loved the things of God, but God Himself alluded me. It was partly by necessity. I had to know God by learning the Bible. That is where God best reveals Himself to us. I loved the idea of God, the comfort of God, the peace of God, the strength of God, the blessings of God, and the gifts of God. I loved what God could do, and had done, for me.

None of that is loving God. It is all about what I can get out of God. The gifts, blessings, and grace made me feel good--primarily about myself--with a nod of gratitude to God. The whole concept of love like that is selfish and selfishly motivated. It puts oneself on the throne and rivals the very God we say we love. God wants us to love Him for Himself, not for His gifts or His blessings. "Delight thyself in the Lord and He shall give thee the desire of thy heart," (Psalm 37:4). "As the hart panteth after the water brooks, so panteth my soul after thee, O God," (Psalm 42:1). "If thou turn away thy foot from the sabbath, from doing thy pleasure on my holy day, and call the sabbath a delight, the holy of the Lord, honourable, and shalt honor him, not doing thy own ways, nor finding thine own pleasure, nor speaking thine own words: Then shalt thou delight thyself in the Lord, and I will cause thee to ride upon the high places of the earth, and feed thee with the heritage of Jacob thy father, for the mouth of the Lord hath spoken it," (Isaiah 58:13-14). Blessings may be a stepping stone, but the goal is to love God for who He is. What ecstasy that brings! Oh, to be satisfied with God!.

We appeal to others for salvation on the basis of their having a better life. We appeal to others for salvation on the basis of Heaven, a mansion, and wonders to behold. We appeal to others for salvation with a warning of Hell. These motives are set before us in Scripture. They are good motives, but they are stepping stones for the carnally minded. They appeal to self--what I get from salvation. The ultimate achievement of salvation leads us to the very presence of God where I want nothing more than Him. The greatest motive is that we shall be like Christ, conformed to His image, seeing Him as He is and so being like Him. The greatest motive is that God's glory is forever manifest by our redemption. The best motive for coming to God is God Himself, not His Heaven or our mansion. Heaven is the by-product of God. It is His home. He deserves no less. We share it with Him, but He is the reason we want to go there. To want nothing more than God Himself--to pant after Him--is the richest and fullest life. That alone reciprocates God's love for us. He sets His affection on us, not for what He may get from us. When He wanted servants, He created angels. When He wanted fellowship, he created man in His own image. Mary, who sat at Jesus' feet, chose the good part that would

not be taken from her.   One thing was needful.
Fellowship is better than service. When the living God
is our only passion we long to be with Him. We want
to talk to Him, to please Him, to sense His presence.
Death we do not see. It is only a stepping stone to our
real passion--the presence of God. To be absent from
the body and present with the Lord is far better for us.
Yet, we find it needful for the furtherance of the Gospel
to abide a little longer in the flesh (II Corinthians 5:4;
Philippians 1:22-24).

I am ready to die. I have had the best life for which
anyone could ask. I have lived my dreams. I started
and managed a Christian radio station. I pastored three
wonderful churches. I have raised a darling daughter
and guided a fine stepson. My wife is my dearest
companion. My best friends and greatest supporters
are my family members. I have traveled the country
and visited the Holy Land (a dream of my youth). I
have done more living than most because I have loved
every minute. Some say they would not like to go back
and live life over again, but I would. The bad things
that happened are so overshadowed by the good things

and life itself is so wonderful that I would do it all over again just for the pleasure of living.

I don't know exactly when or how it happened. But, I can say I am happier now than ever before in my life. I was saved at the age of nine. It has been a steady pace of maturing in Christ. I have not arrived yet. I see, in myself, more flaws than ever before. But God has made Himself known to me. If He never gives another blessing, I will love Him forever for He is wonderful. The years of maturing through trials, struggles, temptations, harassment, illness, grief, study, and discipline are well worth enduring that I may know Him. To know Him is to love Him. More than ever-- more than anything--I love God!

Addendum No. 1

A Wife's Perspective

By Debi Evans

My husband, the author of <u>Journeys of a Feeble Saint</u>, has asked me to write a final chapter. It is my honor and pleasure to give a personal insight into the life and commitment of this servant of God. Our friendship began in 1971 when we were both juniors in high school. It was nothing more than a mutual friendship in a school where everybody knew everybody. While Olen regularly attended the local Baptist Church, I was hit and miss at church Church attendance was neither encouraged nor discouraged in my home, which was a subtle mixture of Roman Catholicism and Southern Baptist. I was twenty-three years old when Christ came into my heart. I did not even remotely consider a life of ministry. I certainly did not anticipate the extent of God's great mercies or the spiritual battles that would follow.

Several years went by after high school before we met again. By this time Olen had finished seminary and was pastoring his first church. He was preaching a revival at a church a few miles from where I was living and I went to hear him. Not a Christian yet, I basically thought I would go and see this former classmate of mine and see if he could really preach (like I would know if he could not). I do not remember a word of what he preached that night; however, my soul was burdened not knowing whether I would go to Heaven or Hell if I died. For weeks I dealt with this conviction and was quite miserable. Scared to go to sleep one night, I tearfully told God that I believed on His Son and wanted His forgiveness. That's all it took. My heart was flooded with peace and my fears subsided. And I thought, "Wow!"

A few years later Olen asked for my help in his new radio station. I assisted with some of the preliminary office work and, eventually, he asked me to manage the office. Christian radio was a completely new concept to me. Olen never intended to be the day-to-day manager of the station. An individual he had met in college was to be the station manager because of his broadcasting degree and "experience." Call it woman's intuition or call it spiritual discernment, my gut told me things were not all they should be with this gentleman and his wife. They were a fine looking couple, regular in church attendance, and musically talented. But something just did not add up. I took great exception at how they treated people, even Olen behind his back. The station signed on but the money was not there to start paying the bills. This guy's job was to secure programming and commercials and very little was done.

What he did do was sign a contract with a major wire service for daily news feeds. He did not discuss it with Olen and kept the contract at his home. Daily news feeds are not inexpensive and the station was obligated for quite a large monthly payment. At first he stated that the wire service was just a trial run with no obligations. Eventually he confessed he had indeed entered into a contract with them. Olen attempted to discuss the situation with the service's legal counsel but to no avail. They believed that, as the station manager, this gentleman represented the station and his authorization was valid. It was seven years before a settlement was reached and we did not come out on top. But it could have been worse, much worse. The service did settle for a fraction of the contract amount.

Within a few months the station manager and his wife resigned from the station and corporate board. That left Olen and me to do the sales, on-air, production, and general day-to-day management. Money was scarce and we were living on as little as possible. Frankly, I was scared but Olen was always faithful in his outlook, never blaming God. He worked the long hours, very often sleeping on the floor of his office.

Our friendship continued to grow and we realized that we loved one another. One evening in an almost unheard of event of "going out to eat," he proposed in a special place that as children we had both gone on numerous occasions. Deming Park in Terre Haute, Indiana, was a place we had separately enjoyed while growing up. Terre Haute was my stomping grounds as a child and I still have a lot of family living there. I accepted his proposal and we were married the following October.

We had an inexpensive wedding and brief honeymoon, thanks to a money tree wedding shower from our friends. Our days were long, leaving at 4:30 a.m. to sign on the station and usually getting home at 7:00 or 8:00 each evening. We did this at least five days a week, sometimes six or seven days. Most of the time when an employee called off at the station, one of us would cover it. It was usually Olen. I remember working eighteen hours straight one Saturday doing on-air coverage. I was so mentally exhausted that I could barely sleep once I finally arrived home. My son, Chris, who was nine years old at the time, was with me the entire day. Olen was preaching a revival that weekend and was unable to help when an employee called in.

I'm here to tell you that I did my share of complaining. Olen accepted the long hours with rarely a complaint, working himself to a point of exhaustion time and time again. This, of course, is not an official diagnosis, but Olen was an over-achiever, a perfectionist. He would refuse to ever ask for help, instead pushing and driving himself and sometimes me. You see, his heart was with the work God had led him to do in establishing a Christian radio station. I did not share this leading in the same capacity. Don't get me wrong! I am a hard and dedicated worker and I love Christian music, but it did not mean the same to me. I wanted more time at home. I did not want the grueling schedule that we had. And, I wanted to see a little more income.

God blessed us with a daughter who was born in July of 1986. It was a difficult pregnancy and I was on complete bed rest for several weeks prior to finally being admitted to the hospital for toxemia. These days the correct terminology is "pregnancy induced hypertension," but it put my life and the life of our unborn child at great risk. I had been in the hospital a week when I had an emergency cesarean section late one night. The doctors were expecting the worst since I had deteriorated rapidly in just a few hours; however, the Great Physician was in control (as He always is).

Our daughter was born healthy and I regained my health quickly.

At the time our daughter was born, Olen was studying for his Doctor of Ministry degree. Studying the Scriptures is his life. One would think that with this degree of education he would move on to greener pastures and certainly a more lucrative one. Former professors and colleagues have told him as much. Olen's pastoral directions come totally from God and not from man. God has placed him to minister in rural areas. He educates himself not only to better teach and preach the Word of God, but to feed and nourish his soul. He doesn't preach for monetary benefit either. He has always accepted what a church believed God led them to give him. Remember I told you that especially in the early years of our marriage money was not plentiful at all. One time Olen was asked to do week-long revival services with the drive one hundred miles round trip. When the revival ended he was not paid so much as gas mileage. You got it! I complained big time. His answer was that God would take care of it at another time. He wasn't concerned at all. Boy, did I have lessons to learn about the Lord's faithfulness. So, at this point in his life his plate was pretty full. A stepson, a new daughter, a business that he worked daily, a bi-vocational church, and pursuit of his doctorate degree. This guy was busy and that's exactly how he liked it.

When Olen started experiencing fatigue and weakness, we just thought it was his work schedule. Blood work revealed kidney failure and a specialist told us a kidney transplant would happen in a few years. Well, it's been fifteen years and the kidneys continue to slowly deteriorate. One kidney is non-functioning and the other has less than 15% function. He has been on the transplant list for the second time for five years now. In the early to mid 1990's, Olen was stricken with other serious health problems. He was diagnosed with a bone marrow disorder, etiology unknown, and he stopped making blood. For several years he had blood transfusions every four to six weeks. Illness, whether chronic or acute, causes individuals and families a great deal of stress. How easy it is not to cast our every care on Him. The stress was great. Olen owned a business, was pastoring a church, finishing his degree, and just daily life in general would soon take its toll.

Something else was going on at that time that is difficult to talk about and explain. Harassment, physically, mentally, and spiritually took place. While we think we know the origin of the harassment now, it was several years before we put the pieces together. A phone call from a woman telling us she hated Baptist preachers and informing us to know the whereabouts of our blonde-headed little girl because she did, pretty much started the harassment. Numerous calls, invasions to our home, the slashing of our outside dog's throat, and the mysterious death of two previous outside dogs (a collie and bird dog) started this roller coaster that lasted a couple of years. These were just some of the physical problems. The effect mentally, especially on Olen who seemed to be the target, was just as difficult. However, this is when I grew spiritually the most because all I had was God on whom to depend. I could not depend on church members, friends, or even some family. We do have friends that were a wonderful support to us in every way; however, they lived in other states. But they were tremendous prayer warriors, lifting us up to God to protect and help us in every way. Their friendship and prayers were encouraging and strengthening. We were involved in a spiritual battle that required the whole armor of God. I cannot begin to describe the emotional distress that all of this involved, especially for Olen. Already in a precarious health situation, Olen suffered a breakdown. It was severe and recovery was long. His health has never been the same.

One thing that Olen and I know is that life has unexpected ups and downs. It may be medical, financial, and spiritual, but what a wonderful God we serve. We both grew as a result of intense struggles. I know I grew more than Olen, because he was already stronger in the Lord. Many years ago, before his health broke, Olen preached a message one Sunday evening from the book of Job. In that message, as he shared the life of Job, he said that he would love and serve God no matter what. If he lost everything, finances and health, and if God chose to test him spiritually, he would still serve Him. Olen's faith never wavered. His health failed and we struggled financially, but never one time did he ask, "Why me?" There were only two questions he presented to the Lord. One was, "What would You have me learn from this?' The other question came after Olen was given six months to live. He asked God to let him see his daughter graduate from high school. She was seven years old at the time and in May of 2004 she graduated and is currently enrolled in business college. Olen gave the address at her class baccalaureate and Sara shared her testimony in word and song. Olen did not know if God would allow him this request. He told God his heart's desire and God gave us assurance that no matter what might happen, it would be right and we would all be okay. How He has blessed us!

What is the end result of this feeble saint? I don't have the complete answer to that. But what I do know is this, God has unfolded a miracle before our eyes, physically and spiritually. While Olen's health still suffers, he is a man of different character in many respects. The before Olen was work driven, a perfectionist, an over-achiever with an intense focus on whatever he was doing. At times he was selfish and demanding. The man I know today is laid back and easy going. He is very supportive of me and puts our family first. The material things of life are not important, but then they never were. The church where we have been for the past nineteen years has never failed in their goodness to us. The members of First Baptist Church in Brownstown are just one of God's blessings in our lives. After nineteen years, they still love their pastor. It was during the roughest years that our church grew the most, both in numbers and in spirit and contentment that has only come about in the last couple of years.

Olen is truly thankful for the longevity of life with which God has blessed him. Through the trials of life, he found a happiness in the Lord that is wonderfully evident. In a similar way, like King David, Olen is a man after God's own heart. His life is God, family, and church. He is relentless in his study of God's Word and is becoming somewhat of a living legend in the pursuit of just the right number of theology books one should possess. He loves his family, his church, his community, his friends, and his neighbors. Most of all he loves God with a passion that is indescribable. He has not only a servant's heart, but a servant's attitude.

This heart and attitude developed and matured over time in God's way. Olen can't wait to meet God. But until he does, he will live this life in service, thankful for the mercies of our faithful Lord.

Addendum No. 2

Journey to Happiness

Comedians make you laugh. Games are fun to play. Financial freedom provides contentment. Entertainers elicit excitement. Friends provide companionship. All of this together cannot produce happiness within you.

Happiness is of the Lord. It cannot be found in a pill or a bottle. In the Beatitudes (Matthew 5:3-12), Jesus promised happiness. The term 'blessed' means 'happy.' It is promised to the poor in spirit, to those who mourn, and even to the reviled and the persecuted. Happiness from the Lord is not based upon living the good life or having a good day.

The Hebrew people used the term 'shalom.' It meant hello, goodbye, and essentially "God bless you." Shalom is translated 'peace.' Peace is more than the absence of conflict. It is the positive affirmation of well-being. Jesus said, "My peace I leave with you, my peace I give unto you, not as the world giveth, give I unto you," (John 14:27).

The world gives temporal pleasures. They who are of the world live for thrills one night at a time, one after the other. They endure life until the weekend, live without a purpose, and achieve nothing of value in their whole life. They grab for the gusto and embrace the philosophy, "if it feels good, do it." The world gives panaceas of joy that last momentarily. Jesus taught that we might have His joy fulfilled within us (John 17:13). In Christ we have real peace (John 16:37). The world cannot take His peace away, neither does it fade away. Temptations, hardships, and even failures only draw us closer to the source of peace -- the Prince of Peace. Jesus promised abundant life (John 10:10). Peter spoke of "joy unspeakable and full of glory" (I Peter 1:8).

To obtain this joy and peace you are required to die to yourself. Paul said, "I die daily" (I Corinthians 15:31). Mark affirmed, "He that loseth his life shall find it" (Mark 8:35). A soldier is valiant in battle and brave because he counts himself already dead. He lives only for the victory he is committed to win. No circumstance is too dangerous because he has nothing left to lose. He is strictly GI -- government issue. He belongs to the cause of his nation, not to himself.

You must cease looking for happiness in the things you do and do not do. Life is not about you -- what you want, what you like, who you are, or what you accomplish. It is not about taking care of number one. Life is all about the Kingdom of God. "Seek ye first the Kingdom of God and His righteousness, and all these things shall be added unto you" (Matthew 6:33).

The world has trained us to believe that we must take care of the necessities of life first. Satan deceives us into believing we must provide for a home, food, and clothing before anything else. With whatever remains, we may choose to support our church, missions, and benevolent causes. Jesus taught just the opposite.

"Therefore I say unto you, Take no thought for your life, what ye shall eat, or what ye shall drink; nor yet for your body, what ye shall put on. Is not the life more than meat, and the body than raiment? Behold the fowls of the air: for they sow not, neither do they reap, nor gather into barns; yet your heavenly Father feedeth them. Are ye not much better than they? Which of you by taking thought can add one cubit unto his stature? And why take ye thought for raiment? Consider the lilies of the field, how they grow; they toil not, neither do they spin: And yet I say unto you, That even Solomon in all his glory was not arrayed like one of these. Wherefore, if God so clothe the grass of the field, which to day is, and to morrow is cast into the oven, shall he not much more clothe you, O ye of little faith? Therefore take no thought, saying, What shall we eat? or, What shall we drink? or, Wherewithal shall we be clothed? (For after all these things do the Gentiles seek:) for your heavenly Father knoweth that ye have need of all these things. But seek ye first the kingdom of God, and his righteousness; and all these things shall be added unto you. Take therefore no thought for the morrow: for the morrow shall take thought for the things of itself, sufficient unto the day is the evil thereof" (Matthew 6:25-34).

Your first priority concerns spiritual needs. It is God's responsibility to supply your physical needs. He who knows your needs before you ask (Matthew 6:8) is the One who promises to sustain you.

Maybe you wished you loved God more than you do. Perhaps you do not feel much attraction to Him. Your heart is just not spiritually inclined to worship Him. Matthew teaches you how to overcome this in 6:21: "For where your treasure is, there will your heart be also." If you want to love God more, give God more. If you are cool toward missions, warm your heart by giving to missions. If you want to love your enemies, your neighbor, or your spouse, give to them. "Do good to those who despitefully use you (Matthew 5:44). If you want to yearn for eternity and Heaven, lay up for yourselves treasures in Heaven (Matthew 6:20). Someone has observed: "You cannot take it with you, but you can send it ahead."

You are not your own, you are "bought with a price. Therefore glorify God in your body and in your spirit which are God's" (I Corinthians 6:20). Your life is hid with Christ in God (Colossians 3:3). The origin and source of eternal life is Heaven. Set your affections on things above. That will create happiness within you.

The joy of which I write is not a passing fancy. It is not just a thrill you may experience upon the first realization that you have been forgiven. Some people are satisfied when God squeezes in a miraculous response to a special prayer. The overwhelming joy of which I speak is the byproduct of walking with God, feeding from His Word, and praying without ceasing. Joy came to me as a gift. I spent years serving from a sense of duty. The joy I had was limited to periods of successful service or emotional experiences of worship. As helpful as those periods may be, they are not the joy you receive from a relationship with Jesus.

For me, a relationship with Jesus means a daily study of God's Word. The Bible is more than a utility manual for godly conduct although godly conduct in itself nurtures some joy. The living Word is a gourmet dinner for body and soul. My schedule prioritizes systematic study for my own personal growth. It goes beyond the necessary study for sermons and lessons. Even though it is personally profitable, study that climaxes in a formal presentation is a dutiful exercise. That kind of study is not the basis of my life with God. The systematic study of God's Word nourishes my soul. I look forward to the spiritual nourishment and crave it spiritually as much as my physical body expects to find nourishment in a fine meal. Rigorous study began as a discipline. As it began to nourish my soul, I found myself living in a state of joyous anticipation for it.

Service is a privilege, not a duty, when you walk with the Lord. "I would rather be a doorkeeper in the house of the Lord than dwell in the tents of the wicked" (Psalm 84:10). The highest position for which you can aspire is to be a servant of God. He is the highest Being. He is infinite and excellent. No one can conceive of anything better. He is the ultimate. He is the Holy of Holies.

To be a servant of God is far more noble than to be a king of worldliness. Service to God is far from degrading. It is honorable. Public servants - politicians - are not considered lower class citizens. Servants of the wealthy class are proud of their station. How much more are we exalted to be servants and sons of God. God's servants are honored above the wisest men of the world. It is a privilege to give a cup of cold water in Jesus' name. It is a privilege to relieve the afflicted for Jesus' sake. It is highest honor to be entrusted with the word of reconciliation (II Corinthians 5:19).

I was happy at the birth of my baby. I was happy at my seminary graduation. I was happy at my wedding. I am happy when I turn a profit. None of this compares to the sensation in my breast that comes from knowing my risen Saviour. He indwells me and fills me with joy.

I encourage you to surrender your life, which is temporal anyway, to gain His resurrection life which never ends. The secret to happy servanthood is complete surrender. Quit trying to get your way. "There is a way that seems right to a man but the end thereof are the ways of death" (Proverbs 14:12). You do not have to wait until you get to Heaven to possess eternal bliss. The joy of the Lord is offered to you in this life as well as in the next life. Ask God for it. He may begin the process by burning away some dross. Some things in your life may be interfering with your spiritual progress. Believe it or not, your personality may need to be overhauled. You will probably be surprised at what all God dredges from your soul when you surrender to Him. Let God mold and shape you. The path to bliss leads through tribulation, but tribulation works patience, and patience, experience, and experience hope, and hope makes no shame (Romans 5:3-5). James adds, "Knowing this, that the trying of your faith worketh patience. But let patience have her perfect work, that ye may be perfect and entire, wanting nothing" (James 1:3-4).

Happiness comes from being in the presence of the Lord. While God is present everywhere and cannot be contained in buildings or objects of creation, He also refers to and manifests Himself in a localized form. He appeared in the Old Testament as the Angel of the Lord. He was in the burning bush of Exodus 3 and the pillar of fire in Exodus 13. He was the smoke of the temple in Isaiah 6. Adam and Eve were accustomed to God's visit in the cool of the day (Genesis 3) and God came down to see the city and tower of Babylon in Genesis 11. More than this, Jesus lives in our hearts. The Lord's presence is often felt at religious meetings. Of course, there is no place where God is not, but you especially sense His presence on specific occasions and it gives you great joy, thrill, and a sensation of spiritual ecstasy.

There is a sense of the Lord's nearness when the saints assemble, pray, worship, study Scripture, or serve as unto the Lord. A conscious awareness of the presence of God provides joy all day long. This sensation is not just the good feeling you get when you have been benevolent, helpful, or an inspiration to others. It is more deep seated and permanent. It is life changing. It is not feeling close to God. It is being close to God. It is not emotional. It is positional. This joy from deep within is a conscious sense of the Lord's approval on your whole life, not just certain isolated actions. As Fanny Crosby wrote: "Redeemed and so happy in Jesus. No language my rapture can tell: I know that the light of His presence with me doth continually dwell." Albert A. Ketchum knew the sentiment when he wrote:

"Deep in my heart there's a gladness; Jesus has saved me from sin: Praise to His name what a Saviour cleansing without and within!"

Knowing this joy motivates you to nurture your soul in Jesus' presence. The happy soul does not invite sin into his life, give place to the devil, satisfy sensual appetites, or flirt with temptation. Vexing your righteous soul with worldly entertainment is frustrating to the Spirit of holiness. It robs you of your joy. I suggest that you avoid modern sit coms on television and movies that contain language and content unbecoming of Christ. Music suitable for the bar room is hardly edifying for a believer. You encounter enough unavoidable offense in the real world without inviting it into your life through fictional characters in your personal entertainment. Do you condemn others who indulge in a more lenient lifestyle? Not at all. Will you be happier for avoiding such amusement? Absolutely!

Why give up your comfort and your desires to do what Christ wants? Why can you not just be yourself? First of all, God is worthy of your allegiance. You have missed the mark and are depraved in nature and you need to be redeemed. Secondly, it is in obedience to Him that you find real rest and refreshment. Vacations and idle time cannot do what Christ does for you. Jesus encouraged His disciples to come apart and rest for a while (Mark 6:31). Certainly, Jesus took periods of rest, but He did not cease His relationship with the Father. He was preparing Himself for further service.

The motivation for service should not be for personal benefits. Your motivation must be to glorify God. You do not serve God for the purpose of obtaining joy for yourself anymore than you give your money in hopes of seeing it returned one hundredfold. Finding joy comes from being lost in the world of God. It is not a trade off. Joy is a gift.

Yes, there are hardships to face, difficulties to endure, grief and miseries to bear. In the song, <u>I Will Sing the Wondrous Story</u>, Francis H. Rowley penned the words: "Days of darkness still come o'er me, sorrows paths I often tread. But the Saviour still is with me: By His hand I'm safely led." There are times, as with Job, you may curse the day of your birth and long to exist no more. In the Nazi concentration camps the fortunate ones were those who died. During intense suffering, death appears inviting. To just cease being would be a blessing in some circumstances. Many who suffer from illness and age would rather be taken in death.

The joy of the Lord that follows suffering is worth all the pain. Job was so satisfied with God that even in the midst of His suffering he could exclaim, "Though He slay me, yet will I trust Him" (Job 13:15). Scripture likens adversity to a woman giving birth. The baby is worth all the pain and mother is willing to go through it all again to have another child.

Many believers throughout the world suffer greatly for their faith. Some are in prison. Something inside of them -- the love of Christ -- is worth keeping the faith. They have given up the rights to their life for Christ's sake and the Gospel's. Joseph was mistreated and imprisoned. Job suffered the loss of everything -- children included. Millions of believers have endured torture and martyrdom. Happiness results from a deliberate dedication to godliness. It is the result of an intentional decision.

God can -- and does -- restore the years the canker worm has eaten. Life is not all joy, all the time. Feelings themselves come and go. Even in trial "the joy of the Lord is my strength" (Nehemiah 8:10). "Count it all joy when you fall into diverse temptations," (James 1:2). The world cannot take the believer's joy from Him. In heartbreak there is also peace so that you "sorrow not even as others who have no hope," (I Thessalonians 4:13).

I have never been drunk. I have never been high. I have never altered my mental state. I am having too much fun with life in Christ to mess it up with attempts at artificially stimulated happiness. What I have from Christ is real, natural, and lasting. "The Lord is my shepherd. I shall not want," (Psalm 23;1). I need nothing in addition to Him.

I was confronted by an older gentleman at church some years ago. He challenged me to show him one place in the Bible that said we should find pleasure in this life. I perceived readily that he had little pleasure in his life. His wife had been confined to a nursing home. He had suffered financial reversal. Although he professed faith in Jesus, he knew little of God. This man was not the first of his kind. Asceticism and stoicism have attracted a following for centuries.

In response to his proposition, the Bible teaches that the whole world is created for man's pleasure. All creation was designed to suit man's needs. The world is for the enjoyment of all mankind. It is perfectly suited for abundant living. God pronounced it good on each day of creation and of the whole He said it is very good. Adam and Eve were placed in a garden, not a wilderness. God is a good God. He expects you to enjoy the fruit of your labor, love your family and friends, know and enjoy Him forever, and worship in the beauty of His holiness.

No, you do not depend on pleasure as an exchange from God for your services. You are bound by duty as well as honor to serve Him. He is King. He is sovereign. He is Lord. We serve Him because of who He is. But, Jesus went beyond duty when He said, "I have called you friends," (John 15:15). If there was no pleasure in service it would still be our obligation to serve.

Yet, serving does promote joy. It is like eating. You have to do it but it is sheer pleasure to taste food. You were created to praise God and serve Him. You were fashioned for a purpose and you are happiest when you function according to your designated end. You ought to seek God's good pleasure. He who put a love for pleasure within you fulfills your passion with His own benevolence. You are required to breathe but God not only supplies you with air, He also instills fragrance. Even though you have to nourish yourself, food is saturated with flavor.

It is within your capacity to find pleasure in a gorgeous sunset, a flower garden, a majestic mountain range, a lovely snowfall, a child's laughter, and a gentle smile. How can an infinite number of blessings not be seen as a pleasure. Surely, you have to work at it to be grumpy, sad, and depressed (barring a physical problem). "A merry heart doeth good like a medicine," (Proverbs 17:22). In Ecclesiastes 8:15 we read ". . . a man hath no better thing under the sun than to eat, and to drink, and to be merry: for that shall abide with him of his labor the days of his life which God giveth him under the sun." Proverbs 5:18-19 adds: "Let thy fountain be blessed and rejoice with the wife of thy youth. Let her be as the loving kind and pleasant roe; let her breasts satisfy thee at all times and be thou ravished always with her love." Paul went further when he admonished Timothy to "charge them that are rich in this world that they be not high minded, nor trust in uncertain riches, but in the living God who giveth us richly <u>all things to enjoy</u>," (I Timothy 6:17).

I may have little of this world's goods, but I lack nothing. "My cup runneth over," (Psalm 23;5). I have everything. I have never heard a dying man wish for more money. I have never heard the dying say he wished he had worked longer hours, had a nicer home, or traveled more widely. I have never heard the dying say he wished he had spent less time with his spouse and children and lived more for himself.

What really matters in life is your relationships. All relationships are based on what you think of God and what you have done with Christ. Jesus puts the zest in living. He is the plumb line by which all relationships are measured and treasured (Matthew 12:46-50). I am confident that no one has ever come to the end of his life and said, "I wish I had spent less time with God."

Your relationship with Christ will put you at odds with the world, but you will be 'glad' and 'happy' because your relationship to the Truth is right. A believer ought to despise sin with so much fury that those who conduct evil business and activity persecute him (Matthew 5:10-12). Jesus said that a life marked by persecution for Jesus' sake is the way to real happiness. Because your citizenship is in Heaven, antagonism from the world must not deter you. Stirring up the world only proves that the world hears your message and is rebelling against a standard higher than its own. "We know we are of God and that the whole world lies under the sway of the wicked one," (I John 5:19 HCSB). This is not obnoxious arrogance on the part of God's children. The poor in spirit are humbled by the blessings of God.

Jesus said, "Blessed are you when men shall revile you, and persecute you, and say all manner of evil against you falsely for my sake. Rejoice and be exceeding glad for great is your reward in Heaven for so persecuted they the prophets which were before you,"

(Matthew 5:11-12). You are on earth as an ambassador with a message to proclaim. How you are received is not a consideration that alters your responsibility. Being successful in the Kingdom is all that matters. The friend of the world is an enemy to God (James 4:4). John affirmed that "if anyone love the world, the love of the Father is not in him," (I John 2:15).

A Christian disciple should not expect to be received any differently than the Saviour Himself. Yet Jesus said, "Love your enemies, bless them that curse you, do good to them that hate you, and pray for them which despitefully use you and persecute you that you may be the children of your Father which is in Heaven, for he maketh his sun to rise on the evil and on the good, and sendeth rain on the just and on the unjust," (Matthew 5:44-45).

There is, indeed, a time to mourn (Ecclesiastes 3), but there is also a time to laugh. Should you not be entertained by God-given talent? Nothing is greater than to love and be loved. No one has ever lived that was not loved by God (John 3:16). Reciprocating God's love is all that precludes you from experiencing divine pleasure.

Happiness is not for an elite few who have, by nature, a jolly disposition. Neither is happiness found in idleness. Happiness is not merely the absence of unhappiness. Joy is found in the work of the Lord, not in an escape from it. Jesus invited, "Come unto me all ye that labour and are heavy laden and I will give you rest. Take my yoke upon you and learn of me, for I am meek and lowly in heart and ye shall find rest unto your souls. For my yoke is easy, and my burden is light," (Matthew 11:28-30).

Burnout does not result from doing too much work for the Lord. It comes from doing the work without the Lord. You burn out when you tug at the yoke forcing an unequal pace (independence), or you get out in front of the other yoke-fellow by a step (presumption), or when you try to do the Lord's work without being yoked with Him (legalism--obeying rules rather than being led by the Holy Spirit), or you balk when He begins to pull (rebellion). "Take my yoke . . . and find rest." The rest is in the work. Weariness is in the world. "The way of the transgressor is hard," (Proverbs 13:15). The yoke of Jesus is easy.

Much too often a Christian worker wishes to step down from service for a year or two to "rest." He says he needs a break. Usually, it is a living relationship with Jesus that he needs. He has tried to serve others but failed to nourish himself. Idleness does not build strength. Nehemiah said, "the joy of the Lord is my strength," (Nehemiah 8:10) or as the HCSB translates, "Your strength comes from rejoicing in the Lord." Isaiah 40:31 reads, "But they that wait upon the Lord shall renew their strength; they shall mount up with wings as eagles; they shall run and not be weary; and they shall walk and not faint."

If you long for real life, abundant life, you need the One who said, "I am the resurrection and the life," (John 11:25). He rose from dead in a glorified body to prove what He said. If you want real life, everlasting life, eternal life, put your mortal life aside. "For whosoever will save his life shall lose it, but whosoever shall lose his life for my sake and the gospel's, the same shall save it. For what shall it profit a man if he shall gain the whole world and lose his own soul? Or what shall a man give in exchange for his soul: Whosoever therefore shall be ashamed of me and of my words in this adulterous and sinful generation, of him also shall the Son of Man be ashamed when he cometh in the glory of his Father with the holy angels," (Mark 8:35-38). If you find it difficult to speak of your faith, you are lacking the personal, daily relationship with Jesus which brings joy and confidence.

True happiness comes from being in the presence of the Lord. "Pray without ceasing," (I Thessalonians 5;17). Never leave the conscious presence of Jesus. In the Lord's presence you can not be consumed with yourself--not even with your fears. "Perfect love casts out fear," (I John 4:18). You are manifest to be poor in spirit. The majesty of His presence clarifies the lowliness of the sinner's own stature. His infinite holiness manifests one's utter sinfulness. All mankind is poor in spirit with nothing to offer, yet in this state Jesus pronounces the believer blessed, or happy (Matthew 5:3). Even when the believer mourns he is happy (Matthew 5:4). This is a paradox to the world, but to those who possess both a sin nature and a Divine nature, it is readily understandable. His strength is made perfect in weakness (II Corinthians 12:9). "When I am weak, then am I strong," (II Corinthians 12:10).

God makes me happy. It is not my happiness that an act of God awakens in me. It is not that I get happy when I think about God or godly things. It is not that some enjoy religion as others enjoy sports, academics, hobbies, or delicacies. God instills happiness in me as a gift. Happiness can be your gift also.

Life is not about you or me. It is not even about family. A spouse is someone within whom you pour the love of Christ. Marriage is a picture of Christ and the church. Life is all about God. He delights in His love. Is godliness a kill-joy? Do you suppose God is unhappy because He is God? Do you think He grumbles at being holy? Do you believe He must force Himself to be good? Nonsense! God is completely fulfilled in Himself. He is all and in all. He is perfect joy.

Even before time, the Father was completely fulfilled in His love for His Son. Jesus was and is the brightness of God's glory and the express image of His person

(Hebrews 1:3). There is nothing--no one--greater than He. He is perfect excellency. He can and He must delight in Himself. He bids you to delight yourself in Him, "Looking unto Jesus, the author and finisher of our faith, who for the joy that was set before him, endured the cross, despising the shame, and is set down at the right hand of the throne of God," (Hebrews12:2).

About the Authors

Olen Evans has served as pastor of the First Baptist Church in Brownstown, Illinois, since 1986. He and his wife Debi have two adult children. Olen was named outstanding smaller church Pastor of the Year for the Eastern Half of the United States in 2001 by Lifeway of the Southern Baptist Convention. He earned an A.S. degree from Lincoln Trail College in Robinson, Illinois; a B.A. in Bible from Tennessee Temple University and an M.Div. in theology from Temple Baptist Theological Seminary, both in Chattanooga, Tennessee; and D.Min. in pastoral studies from Luther Rice Seminary now in Atlanta, Georgia.

Debi is a Registered Nurse employed as Patient Care Manager of Fayette County Hospital of Vandalia, Illinois.

The authors can be reached at debrn54@frontiernet. net

Printed in the United States
38750LVS00001B/310-471